Everything you
need to know

about
gardening
but were afraid to ask

Rob Cassy and
Valerie Scriven

Everything you need to know

about
gardening

but were afraid to ask

FRANCES LINCOLN

To Anne Robbins and Ruth Swindon
for their love and friendship
R.C.

For Dominic, Amanda and my grandchildren
V.S.

Frances Lincoln Limited
4 Torriano Mews
Torriano Avenue
London NW5 2RZ

Everything you need to know about gardening
but were afraid to ask

British Library Cataloguing in Publication Data

A catalogue record for this book is available from
the British Library

ISBN 0 7112 1978 8

9 8 7 6 5 4 3 2 1

Printed and bound in Hong Kong

Contents

Gardens are for everyone

The cultivation of crops and flowers represents both
primitive man's need to tame the wilderness
and civilized man's quest for Arcadia.
Whether your garden is a pot on a sill,
an urban enclave or a country retreat,
it is your window to the world
and a mirror to your soul.

'*Il faut cultiver notre jardin.*'

— Voltaire, *Candide*, 1759

We need plants.

All living things require sugar for energy. Plants manufacture their own sugar. They do this through a process known as photosynthesis. Plants absorb moisture from the soil through their roots and carbon dioxide from the air through pores in their leaves. Light energy harnessed by the green leaf pigment chlorophyll breaks water molecules down into hydrogen and oxygen, chemically combining the hydrogen with the carbon dioxide to form sugars for the plant and releasing pure oxygen into the air as a by-product. Animals on the other hand — including humans — depend on plants for food, which they convert into sugar, either directly as herbivores or indirectly as carnivores.

Not only do plants feed us, but by producing oxygen and absorbing carbon dioxide they harmonize the earth's atmosphere, balancing out the living processes of animals and mankind who breathe oxygen in and carbon dioxide out.

So much for the science. Long before we knew all this there was one thing early man understood only too well: hunger. It was purely as a

previous page The closer you look, the more amazing they seem. Sunlight, water and fresh air are almost all that plants need. If only human life were as simple. Wherever you live, whatever you do, get back to nature with some sort of gardening.

source of food that plants were initially put under cultivation. Ground was cleared of unwanted plants to make room for beneficial ones. From being a nomadic hunter-gatherer man came to lead a more sedentary existence, forming communities to nurture and protect fruit, grains and vegetables. Eventually, seed was sown and crops could be relied upon. As civilization flourished, attention could finally be paid to the aesthetic qualities of plants, and the skills which had been developed through farming were put to use in creating the first purely decorative gardens.

Today, with everyone striving to improve their quality of life, gardening has come to the fore as a leisure pursuit – not only as a means of visually improving our surroundings and adding value to our homes, but as a way of relaxing and reattuning ourselves to the natural world. Not only are plants and flowers beautiful to look at and therefore spiritually refreshing, but the process of tending them strengthens our bond with the world and makes us feel needed. (As a last resort in the mental health stakes you can of course talk to your plants, but do seek immediate professional help if they ever start talking back.)

We can all close our eyes and visualize our ideal garden. For some people it might be that of a rambling English vicarage with bees humming through jumbles of flowers and ducks running round on the lawn. For others it might be a sophisticated roof terrace for entertaining guests while admiring panoramic city views. Other people might hanker for a lush tropical paradise or the elegant simplicity of a cloistered formal garden with fountains and statues.

But dreaming is one thing and reality is quite another. Many people live in flats or shared houses with no garden to call their own. Others move home so frequently that they never feel it's worth making a start. Yet others think their garden, yard or balcony is so small or has so little promise that they would never attempt to make something of it in a

9

million years. In our largely urban environment the passing on of gardening skills from generation to generation is a haphazard affair at best, and more and more of us come to gardening as complete innocents. For all sorts of reasons people write themselves off as second-class citizens and deprive themselves of the pleasures of a garden.

Well, whatever your abilities, whatever the state of your finances, throw down your chains. If your garden is a constant source of worry to you, lighten up and look at things afresh. After all, plants are the oldest forms of life on earth and they have been looking after themselves in the wild for millions of years without any help from you. True, you might have to wait until you win the lottery to get the garden of your dreams, but until then you can jolly well learn to make the most of what you've got. Even if you haven't got a garden, don't worry: there's plenty you can do without one. You can enjoy gardens without doing a stroke of work by admiring the front gardens you pass in the street, by walking through parks or by visiting botanical gardens and stately homes. You can work in a garden without owning one by helping the little old lady down the road, by doing voluntary work, by renting an allotment or by becoming involved in a community garden.

The secret to getting started is simple. All you need is a positive attitude and, just so long as you don't try to run before you can walk, everything else will simply fall into place. Honest. Let's face it, you've already got a more relaxed attitude to gardening, you understand photosynthesis and you're only halfway through the first chapter.

previous page 'To own a bit of ground, to scratch it with a hoe, to plant seeds and watch the renewal of life – this is the commonest delight of the race, the most satisfactory thing a man can do.' – Charles Dudley Warner, *My Summer in a Garden*, 1870

Gardening is about having a go at things and embracing the opportunities you're presented with. If you think you've got a problem garden you're not alone, but the chances are you're really the proud owner of a unique habitat just waiting to be planted up. And if you can't afford to buy many plants, just learn instead how to propagate them from seeds or cuttings – it's more satisfying anyway. Remember above all else that an ounce of practice is worth a pound of theory, so just get out there and make a start.

One thing leads to another, and just as tending even the most undemanding of houseplants proves to be a useful experience for the neophyte gardener, so the knowledge gained in individual aspects of gardening quickly builds into a fully rounded understanding of gardening as a whole. A little knowledge and experience will enable you to channel your energy directly towards successful outcomes, and that is what this book is all about.

Pots inside and out

*A Grecian urn costs a fortune but a few pence
buy a flowerpot, and that's all you need
to embark on a lifetime's adventure in gardening.
Choose plants for your home according to
the light, heat and humidity you can offer;
use the right compost; feed and water wisely –
and you'll soon be in paradise.
When you're stuck for space indoors,
let your imagination run riot outside
with a colourful profusion of hanging baskets
and window boxes.*

Whether you're the poor man in his hovel or the rich man in his hall you can improve the quality of your life in a matter of days by creating an oasis of tranquillity in your home using houseplants.

Houseplants

Collecting houseplants makes your home infinitely more inviting and is the easiest and cheapest form of interior decoration. Each room can be given a distinctive mood and style by being furnished with plants from different habitats. A steamy bathroom full of ferns, bamboos, bromeliads and large-leaved climbers will evoke a tropical rainforest. A group of agaves, yuccas and cacti in brightly painted containers can transport you to Mexico, while terracotta pots brimming with geraniums and bougainvillea instantly conjure up visions of the Mediterranean.

You will already have worked out that houseplants improve air quality in the home by producing oxygen and absorbing carbon dioxide. What you might not know is that it has now been scientifically proved that houseplants also remove air-borne toxins such as ammonia, benzene, chloroform, formaldehyde and xylene, which are emitted by all electrical appliances and most man-made materials including carpets, plastic wall and floor coverings, ceiling tiles, chipboard and MDF.

As well as having great aesthetic value and giving real physical benefits, houseplants can help us psychologically. Human beings are social animals, but when working long hours or living alone in large towns and cities we can become disconnected from friends and family and cut off

previous page Beautifully planted containers like these giant pots of lilies achieve two things simultaneously. They are miniature gardens in their own right and decorative elements which enhance their surroundings. Indoors or out, potted plants make any area doubly attractive.

from Nature by our increasingly harsh man-made environment. Everyone, and children and elderly people particularly, can benefit from having a few plants around them, especially when they are presents and therefore have emotional connections. You will also find that students leaving home, people moving house and the recently bereaved particularly appreciate houseplants as gifts.

Perhaps it's an obvious thing to say, but the house isn't the natural environment of houseplants. All houseplants started out in the wild, coming from a vast range of different climates and soil conditions, and if they're left alone to fend for themselves they'll die. But giving plants the care and attention they need is immensely rewarding. The more you give your plants the more they will actually thrive instead of just getting by. The better they do, the keener you will be to get more of them and to try your hand with increasingly exotic and unusual varieties. The more plants you look after, the more you will find they do something for you in return.

And learning how to care for plants indoors introduces you to some of the principles of botany and horticulture.

Acquiring plants

The more available a plant is to buy – whether it's for the house or the garden – the more confident you can be that it will be able to get by with the minimum of care. Intrinsic merit is what makes a plant commonplace. The association of 'common' with 'vulgar' is a strange and perverse connection made only in the mystifying world of the gardening snob.

Feel free to prod and poke around when you're buying plants. You're parting with hard-earned money and you have a right to good value whether you're in the grandest of garden centres or the humblest of street markets. Once you get it home, a healthy plant will be off to a flying start while a sickly one will need nursing and cosseting and may even spread

pests and diseases to plants you already have. A poor specimen, however cheap, is always a false economy – so don't even think about it.

A new plant should be sturdy and erect with evenly balanced all-round growth. You also want dense leaf cover, with the leaves perfectly healthy and without the least trace of damage or discoloration. Cacti and succulents should be firm and unblemished, shiny-leaved plants glowing with vigour. Matt or furry-leaved plants should have a uniform appearance and be free of blotches, which can be a sign of rot. You shouldn't buy anything with soft, pale or weak growth on it and the only leggy or dangly plants you want are climbers or trailers. Check that climbers are fastened to their supports but that the clips or ties aren't so tight that they're cutting into the stems. Ensure that the stems of trailers aren't kinked, twisted or otherwise damaged. When presented with a choice of specimens opt for the one with the most stems coming from the base or with the promise of the most young shoots or flower buds.

You will of course graciously receive any plant given as a present – but as soon as the donor is out of sight you should check it over for creepy-crawlies and take any appropriate action before giving it a home.

Light and heat

Light and heat affect the metabolic rate of plants. This in turn affects the rate at which plants lose water, which they do continuously as they use it during photosynthesis and lose it through transpiration – that is, the loss

In cooler climates tender shrubs such as this Latin-American abutilon and climbers like the plumbago or Cape leadwort will reach a decent size and flower so profusely only if growing conditions remind them of their homelands. Well potted, under cover and in good light they'll thrive; outdoors in the ground, one snap of frost and they'll be gone.

19

of water by evaporation through leaf pores. Green plants need sunlight to grow and thrive. They would all die without it, but the quality of light required by each type of plant varies enormously according to how they have adapted to conditions in their native habitat. While agaves, for instance, relish the burning heat and harsh light of the desert sun, shade-loving trilliums thrive in the dappled light filtering through the cool leaf canopy of their woodland home. So it is essential to understand a plant's heat and light needs when you consider the question of where to put it.

All plants, but especially young ones, can be so shocked by sudden extreme changes in temperature that they suffer a check in their growth. Too many shocks and they might just give up the ghost.

Bear this in mind if you're buying houseplants in cold wintry weather. A plant that has been outside all morning, which you buy in the street on your lunch break, take back to a stuffy office for the afternoon, carry home on the train and dump in your centrally heated sitting room will already have been in and out of several chilly lorries and vans on its way from grower to wholesaler to shopkeeper or stallholder. If you've ever bought a poinsettia at Christmas only to have it shed all its leaves overnight, now you know why.

Any plant will thrive best in whichever location has the most in common with its natural habitat. The shrubs of the Mediterranean maquis for instance, such as cistus, genista and Spanish broom, are all naturally drought-tolerant. The nature of the soil is relevant too, but we'll come to that later. You don't need to be too scientific here – make sure you know where a plant comes from and then just use your own eyes and a bit of common sense.

In the case of houseplants, assess which areas of your home are the hottest, the coldest, the sunniest, the gloomiest, the most humid and the driest. Then position your plants accordingly. Simple! Windowsills receiving direct midday sun can become so hot that only desert and Mediterranean plants can survive without baking. Should plants' leaves turn yellow, scorch or even bleach, they should be given the immediate protection of blinds or net curtains or moved somewhere shadier. Windows receiving only indirect sunlight are generally a safe bet, but if leaves turn pale or if growth becomes soft and lanky due to lack of light, plants need moving to a sunnier spot. If choosing plants for the main body of a room, opt for tropicals preferring dappled and filtered light such as forest-floor dwelling aspidistras and spider plants, epiphytic plants such as orchids and bromeliads which grow in pockets of rotting leaf matter on trees, and jungle vines such as devil's ivy and the Swiss cheese plant which grow up towards the leaf canopy. (Purely as an aside, the botanical name for devil's ivy is *Epipremnum*, from the Greek *epi*, meaning upon, and *premnum*, a trunk, referring to its habit in the wild of climbing up trunks. As you will see later, plants' fancy names aren't just plucked out of a hat, and they often tell you a lot about them.) Bear in mind that light levels drop away steeply as you go deeper into a room.

Beware the intense dry heat of radiators and hot air ducting and always position plants well out of drafts from outside doors. The only other temperature threat in modern homes comes from chilly windowsills on winter evenings. The depth of your purse and the extent of your patience will be the deciding factors here. You can keep plants out of danger by installing double glazing, moving them every evening – which is tedious – drawing your curtains between the plants and the window or leaving your curtains open overnight, thereby avoiding frost pockets but raising your fuel bills.

We can't do much about light levels in our homes and we're unlikely to change the heating to increase the comfort of our plants at the expense of our own. The one factor we can realistically control in the immediate vicinity of our houseplants is the humidity. Increasing relative humidity helps plants tolerate higher levels of heat and light than they would otherwise prefer.

Mist spraying is the obvious short-term way to raise air moisture levels, but you have to be careful not to damage furniture and fabrics. A good long-term technique is to sit flowerpots on pebble-filled dishes half-full of water which slowly evaporates in the warmth of a room. Grouping plants together also increases local humidity, creating a microclimate where plants share the water vapour coming from each other's leaves and from the surface of the soil in their pots.

Watering

As water is lost from a plant, it needs to be replaced, so now we come to the vexed question of watering. This is more of an art than a precise science and really needn't be the least source of worry. Plants should simply be watered when they need it and left alone when they don't. By relaxing and keeping a regular eye on your plants you will acquire an instinctive understanding of their needs. If in doubt, poke your finger a centimetre or so into the surface of the soil around the plant and if it is dry or only barely moist, water away. More houseplants die through overwatering than neglect, so if in doubt, don't water but if the plant goes limp or starts to wilt, check the soil immediately. Overwatering leads to waterlogged and rotten roots, the symptoms of which can be mistaken for dryness – leaves wilt then go brown and brittle at the edges. Once you've started overwatering you can get trapped into a vicious cycle which stops only when the plant drops dead. Knowing when to water is a piece of cake once you know how to water.

If you water houseplants frequently and timidly, you're failing to serve their best interests. This approach might dampen the soil surface and the sides of the root ball but it often leaves a permanently dry core in the centre of the pot. Keeping your pots in saucers leads inexorably to this problem. If you water from above you don't dare be too generous in case the water overflows. If you water from below you might never be giving the soil as much water as it can absorb. The best approach is to keep your flowerpots in bowls and cachepots rather than saucers. Pour a generous amount of water into these and wait for it to be absorbed into the soil by capillary action. When the soil is properly wet its upper surface will be glistening, and if there is any water remaining in the bowl at this point you should tip it away. The plant now has sufficient reserves of water to draw on until the soil is dry and another thorough watering is needed. On no account leave a pot sitting in water for any length of time: plant roots need oxygen and doing this will suffocate them.

Houseplants quickly deplete soil nutrients when in active growth so from early spring to late summer it is wise to water with a proprietary fertilizer diluted according to the manufacturer's instructions. During autumn and winter when plants are not actually growing it is better not to feed them as this could lead to a harmful build-up of chemical salts in the soil.

Containers

Without even an inch of ground to their name, anyone can put on a really good show with window boxes and hanging baskets alone. If there's space for a few freestanding pots beside the door, running either side of some steps or in a small basement area, yard or patio, you're really on your way to something special. If you move home frequently, growing in containers is a good way to build up a collection of plants which will provide you with the makings of an instant garden when you finally put down roots.

The choice of pots is easily as important as the choice of plants. Traditional stone and lead are as beautiful as they are expensive — but a big disadvantage here is that despite their enormous weight they do tend to walk in the night. Terracotta comes in a huge range of styles and prices and weathers beautifully over time. Don't be ashamed of plastic — it has other attractions besides economy; however, avoid at all costs the stuff coloured like some unfathomable prosthetic device but masquerading as terracotta — it's ugly enough to start with and gets even worse with age. For a touch of bohemian chic or where thrift is a real driving force it is worth salvaging old buckets (be wary of zinc — it is toxic to some plants), catering-sized tins and plastic drums — even babies' bathtubs and old teapots can be brought into play. All containers need drainage holes, so where necessary be sure to punch or drill adequate drainage holes in such treasures. Over time most people acquire a wide range of different containers and rearrange them as they go, putting new favourites to the front and retiring old stalwarts to the background.

Stone and lead containers protect roots from hot summer sun and cold winter frost while plastic and sheet metal leave plants a little more exposed to the elements. All are excellent at conserving moisture. Unglazed terracotta pots are good insulators; being porous they lose water more rapidly but this 'breathability' helps keep soil fresh and aerated and means you don't need to worry too much about overwatering. Terracotta's enduring popularity with indoor and outdoor gardeners alike is no accident of fate but a well-deserved success story.

Safety should always be a consideration in the garden, and there are a few important things to bear in mind when using containers. Don't place them where people could trip or fall over them. Secure all window boxes firmly in place with metal retaining bars. Low-flying terracotta can be lethal, and although plastic troughs are marginally less likely to brain passers-by their very lightness makes them more prone to flight in the first place. Don't trust anything to luck on balconies or roof terraces where winds can be treacherous – a pot that is well balanced when newly planted can become dangerously top-heavy after a few months of growth, especially when the container itself is lightweight and a peat-based rather than a loam-based compost has been used. Once a hanging basket is in position it is a wise precaution to secure it firmly with wire or string.

Potting compost

The best all-round potting composts to use for both container plants and houseplants are the loam-based ones formulated by the John Innes Institute in the 1930s. They are free-draining, moisture-retentive and well aerated, and contain a steady supply of nutrients. John Innes No. 1 contains relatively little fertilizer, No. 2 has twice as much, and No. 3 has three times the amount. No. 1 is for seedlings and young plants; No. 2 and 3 are for more established and larger, woodier plants. We suggest you just buy No. 3 and have done with it.

While loam-based composts may contain some peat to open up their texture, many modern composts are composed almost entirely of peat or a peat substitute such as coconut fibre with added sand for drainage.

What nutrients these have don't last for long. They are prone to waterlogging and become sour in wet conditions but are hard to re-wet properly once they dry out. Because they are so lightweight, tall plants potted up in them can become precariously top-heavy. While we would prefer not to use peat-based composts – not least for environmental reasons – they do have a place. It is always best to keep a plant in the compost it is accustomed to, and once started off in a peat-based medium roots will forever fight shy of anything loam-based, finding it comparatively harder going. Rather like children who will only eat white sliced bread, plants don't always know what is good for them.

Some plants have very particular needs, and there are a few specialized composts to be aware of:

- *Bulb fibre* – this has a very open structure to allow for good aeration, as bulbs are often grown directly in decorative bowls without drainage holes.
- *Cactus compost* – this is gritty, very free-draining and low in nutrients.
- *Ericaceous compost* – a rich acidic medium for azaleas, camellias, gardenias and other lime-haters. Such plants are best watered with rainwater or boiled tap water cooled to room temperature.
- *Orchid compost* – probably the most unusual compost, this is very coarse, fibrous and free-draining. It can contain bark, fern root fibres, moss and even polystyrene chips.

Planting containers

For maximum impact with a hanging basket, always remember to shove plants through the bottom and sides as you fill up with compost, lightly tucking moss around the outside to hold everything in place. Use a

Never deny a generous impulse. Containers around your home are like jewels for your lover: the bigger and brighter the better. Zinnias, black-eyed Susans and African marigolds jostle for attention in this boldly planted display.

proprietary plastic or sheet fibre liner if you must, but they are much harder to work with and not at all gentle on the eye.

You really can't be too generous when it comes to planting up a window box; the wow factor always comes from a colourful and abundant show rather than a pinched display of restrained good taste. It is here that well-anchored plastic containers win over all others – black or very dark green ones disappear behind the trailing foliage and flowers, and distract the eye less from your planting scheme than terracotta does. The broader a window box the better, as you can then arrange your plants in staggered rows, with the tallest at the back, the bushy ones in the middle and the trailers at the front. Keep the soil depth 2.5cm/1in below the rim of the box to make watering easy and if you must use a drip tray be aware that water can stagnate, leading to sour soil and rotten roots.

Permanent plantings of small trees and shrubs or dramatic architectural evergreens such as bamboos, castor oil plants, cordylines, phormiums and yuccas are best left to large free-standing containers, where they'll have an ample root run and can remain undisturbed for years, rather than hanging baskets and window boxes. Otherwise, because plantings in containers are best regarded as short-term arrangements you are limited only by your imagination and the range of plants you can get your hands on. Any 'mistakes' won't be around to haunt you for long and every planting will be a whole new learning experience. Aim to plant up in late spring for a good summer display and then again in autumn for a winter show; just buy whatever you fancy in the garden centre. Reliable winter performers include dwarf conifers, cyclamen, daphnes, heathers, ivies and the winter cherry (*Solanum capsicastrum*). The more you learn about plants generally the more you'll be able to adapt your choice of container plants to any season or location.

Containers hold relatively little soil considering the number of plants grown in them. It soon dries out and becomes nutrient-depleted, so regular watering and feeding is essential. These chores can be lightened a little by mixing water-retaining gel and slow-release fertilizer granules into the potting medium at the time of planting. A 2.5cm/1in deep plastic saucer put into a hanging basket halfway through planting up will act as a reservoir and help achieve thorough wetting of the compost.

Potting on

A healthy plant or houseplant grown in a container will eventually grow too big for its boots and will need potting on. It is a sure sign that this is necessary when a plant is constantly in need of watering. As a general guide the new pot should allow 2.5cm/1in more space all round. You can get away with less for a really small plant and a really big plant will appreciate a proportionately larger pot. Gently tap the plant out of its old pot, sit it on a layer of compost already in the new pot, and then fill in with compost round the sides, lightly firming as you go. The new compost should be just level with the old. You might want to take it a little higher for aesthetic reasons, but don't overdo this as it can encourage the plant stem to rot. Give the plant a good watering and you're done.

When repotting houseplants keep root damage to a minimum by using a gentle touch. Settle the compost by thumping the pot on the ground a couple of times. Water well, then watch in wonder the ensuing spurt of growth.

There's no such thing as a problem garden

Whether your garden is damp or dry,
shaded from the sun or exposed to the four winds,
an honest appraisal of conditions is the key to
unlocking its hidden potential.
Broaden your horticultural horizons by learning from
Nature which plant adaptations work where and
adopt old gardening wrinkles to outwit the elements
while your selections get established.
Your garden will never look back.

The single greatest piece of gardening advice in history is Alexander Pope's: 'In all, let Nature never be forgot . . . Consult the Genius of the Place.' If you think you've got a 'problem' garden, all you have to do is find the right plant for the right place, while allowing your design to evolve along realistic lines, and you are away.

Garden centres don't label plants for their own entertainment, so if a plant is described as 'good on poor, dry soil' and that's what you have, go for it. Wishful thinking gets you nowhere, so don't tempt fate. 'Prefers a rich, moist soil' means precisely that; don't cart anything home which is doomed to failure from the outset. The simplest route to success is to be guided by what grows well in your neighbours' gardens and to learn from their mistakes. Whenever possible beg, borrow or steal seedlings or divisions of successful plants from neighbours in preference to buying commercially grown specimens. Price isn't the only attraction here. To get as many big healthy plants as quickly as possible, nurseries cosset their tender young charges with the optimum combination of warmth, moisture, food and shelter. This has a tendency to produce top-heavy plants with soft, luxuriant top-growth and roots so accustomed to spoonfeeding that they're not quite up to their job when exposed to the more hostile environment of the real world. A plant from next door, on the other hand, suffers little stress in transportation, it doesn't have to adapt itself to a different type of soil, and it will already be growing in harmony with the prevailing conditions in your garden.

Plants are certainly the most important element in a garden, but they

previous page There's someone for everyone, and there's a plant for every place. Boggy ground in partial shade might sound like a gardener's nightmare but it's the perfect home for yellow skunk cabbage (*Lysichiton americanus*). If its 45cm/18in spring flowers impress you, the 1m/3½ft high leaves which follow on will bowl you over.

are only one part of an overall concept which can include hard surfacing, walls, fences, water, lighting, garden furniture and sculpture. If you allow your design to respond naturally to the requirements of your garden, you will find that the worst places for plants become the best sites for these other elements.

The resourceful gardener can always make a virtue of necessity. While we're in eighteenth-century mood, it is worth considering the example of Pope's own garden at Twickenham. It was divided by a road, so a tunnel was constructed to connect the two parts. Instead of leaving the tunnel as a dank dark passageway, Pope made a feature of it and transformed it into a grotto.

Shady gardens

Let's think for a moment how you could transform your own shady garden. More than any other 'problem' garden, a shady site enables the imaginative gardener to introduce a wide range of dramatic plants and create a really unique atmosphere.

A conventional garden pond could quickly stagnate – collecting leaves, clogging with weed and becoming a breeding ground for mosquitoes. On the other hand, a bubbling fountain playing over pebbles would introduce movement, bring the garden alive with the tinkling sound of water and make it sparkle with reflected light.

If your lawn is a balding and moss-filled nuisance, transform it into a tranquil and easily swept sitting area using stone slabs, cobblestones, tile or pebble mosaics or even wooden decking. If you'd prefer a softer-looking surface which won't become slippery when wet, you could opt instead for a decorative mulch of bark chippings, deliciously chocolate-smelling cocoa husks, gravel, pebbles or broken, coloured glass. These all need laying to a depth of at least 5cm/2in and can easily be maintained by the occasional raking. The very adventurous might even consider a Japanese moss garden with stone slabs or timber rounds for light foot traffic. Moss is one of those things that does largely as it pleases, so if your garden isn't already a natural breeding ground don't even think about it. If it is, and you want to encourage it to spread, you might care to know that paraquat kills all green plants except moss. No more clues! Just remember that all weedkillers are highly toxic and must be used strictly in accordance with the manufacturers' instructions.

While all plants need sunlight, most plants will tolerate light shade, so it is always worth experimenting. With deeper shade it is sensible to choose ones that demand it as their habitat. It is better to have a few thriving and spreading plants than a lot of barely surviving ones.

A traditional rockery won't thrive – alpines quickly become etiolated in poor light, they need good air circulation, and they hate water dripping on them from above. With a little imaginative replanting you could have a fascinating Victorian fernery instead.

If you insist on having plants in those rare places which are so dark that nothing can survive for long, such as alcoves under basement stairways, you can cheat Nature by rotating your containerized plants, giving each one a week's tour of duty before returning it to its home base for rest and recuperation.

Shade lovers generally bloom in late winter and in spring before light levels are reduced by the summer leaf canopy, and they have often

In the deep shade of this atmospheric wooded dell young gunnera stalks hold their 'giant rhubarb' leaves aloft as skunk cabbage greenery unfurls behind them in the dappled light of overhanging branches. The sword-like foliage of a flag iris cuts into a swathe of hostas in the clearing and a thuggish rodgersia lurks ominously by.

evolved either relatively large leaves or graceful arching stems to help them capture as much light as possible. Coming mostly from a woodland setting they prefer a loose, leafy-textured soil, so whether your shade is caused by trees or adjacent buildings you can always improve your plants' living conditions by importing as much organic matter as possible.

White-, cream- or yellow-variegated foliage not only introduces year-round colour but when artfully placed it can create an illusion of sunlight spilling into your garden. Lime-green leaves or floral bracts, for example of plants such as *Euphorbia amygdaloides*, *Philadelphus coronarius* 'Aureus' and *Smyrnium perfoliatum* can be particularly helpful in this respect and the evergreen *Choisya ternata* 'Sundance' and *Hedera helix* 'Buttercup' are positively invaluable. Many variegated plants suit shade because, like fair-skinned people, they scorch easily in full sun. It's worth keeping an eye on yellow-leaved plants though – too shady a spot and they revert to green.

Dry gardens

It's surprisingly easy to rattle off a list of adjectives which singly or in combination will perfectly describe any plant well adapted to surviving drought. Silvery, mealy, hairy, furry, filigree, gummy, glaucous, grey, aromatic, strappy, leathery, scaly, spiky, woolly, spiny, needle-like, succulent, fleshy. The drier and sunnier your garden the more you should seek out plants with these characteristics if you want to keep watering and routine maintenance to a minimum and if you want your selections to grow and thrive year on year. Armed only with this information any gardening neophyte could visit a well-stocked nursery or garden centre and come away with several carloads of plants perfectly suited to conditions in a dry garden. Let's look at a few examples. Rosemary and lavender have aromatic, silvery needle-like leaves, the small surface area of which drastically cuts loss of water through transpiration. The furry silver-grey 'wool' on *Stachys byzantina* not only protects the leaves, stems and flowers from the glare of the sun and the desiccating effects of the wind but helps trap moisture close to the leaf surface. If drooping under stress, the glaucous leathery leaves of the eucalyptus have the astonishing ability to turn edgewise to the sun, presenting the smallest possible surface area to its fierce heat. The succulent, fleshy leaves of houseleeks ... you get the point. Below ground, a sturdy tap-root, bulbs and rhizomes are all good indicators of plants able to hold their own in dry conditions.

Don't automatically assume that plants with large green leaves are entirely off the agenda. True, they tend to transpire copiously in full sun so are generally better adapted to life in either the shady garden or the damp garden, but some have drought-defying characteristics which make them welcome and trouble-free additions to the dry garden. Not only do the bergenia's waxy and leathery saucer-like leaves seal water in and deflect the sun's glare, but they are so densely packed together that they keep the soil below cool and moist. In a two-pronged campaign against drought the elegant acanthus presents shiny, cut-away leaves to the sun and a tough, vigorous root system to the ground. Mature specimens of the ludicrously oversized sea kale cousin *Crambe cordifolia* not only shade the soil with their leaves (killing off local competition in the process), but their massive tap-roots source water from deep underground which is quite beyond the reach of your average garden inhabitant. Throughout Nature, size and thuggery always make a winning combination.

Those of you who were paying attention in the previous chapter will now realize that plants grown in a peat-based compost are particularly prone to failure in the dry garden because their roots are disinclined to venture beyond the existing root-ball and because peat dries out so

quickly and is difficult to re-wet.

Just as some plants are better than others at fighting drought, so are certain gardening practices. Care of the soil and generous mulching are what really count in the long term. Frequent watering is the most obvious but least efficient response: plants become addicts, gardeners become slaves. Plants that are fed and watered with a heavy hand will grow lush and verdant while their disproportionately small roots loiter idly for the rich pickings at the soil's surface. Such plants are like spoilt children living beyond their means: they have no reserves to draw on in times of need and are quickly brought to their knees in a crisis. On the other hand plants accustomed to lean living will develop an extensive root system and will only put on as much top-growth as they can comfortably support.

Caring for the soil so that it's as moisture-retentive as possible is what will really count in the long term. So will gradually reducing the frequency of your watering but increasing the volume you apply when you do water. A good drenching will penetrate the soil more deeply and encourage roots to follow. At the same time cut back on any artificial feeding and begin mulching around plants instead to conserve water, starting with the most vulnerable and working your way round to the toughest. Transplant anything that is clearly suffering to a naturally shadier or damper part of the garden. If a few plants die, they die. At the end of a season's regime of tough love you'll be a happier gardener with a healthier garden, and if you've got a space or two to fill, just run through our helpful list of adjectives as you trot off down the shops.

previous page Requiring no watering at all, this dry sunny garden overflows with the finely cut grey and silver foliage of rosemary, lavender and artemisia. The soaring yellow verbascum has a belt-and-braces approach to drought: its leaves are covered in fur to prevent moisture loss and its tap-root plunges deep into the earth in search of water.

Windy and seaside gardens

We all know the effect of a harsh wind on our faces. Never underestimate its destructive potential in the garden. Trees, shrubs and tall flowering plants are prone to stem damage and root rock as they are buffeted around. The rapid airflow around leaves increases transpiration; particularly fierce or prolonged gales can leave them desiccated.

Creating an effective shelterbelt is essential. Solid boundaries like walls are not the ideal windbreaks you might imagine: in strong gales air turbulence on the leeward side can be even more damaging to plants than direct horizontal wind and only plants at the very foot of the wall get any protection at all. Semi-permeable screens of fencing, trees and shrubs, on the other hand, are ideal: the force of the wind is reduced for a distance of up to twenty times the height of the screen and the most sheltered area lies within a distance eight times the height of the screen. A light fence can be erected instantly, providing immediate protection for the garden as a whole and for a mixed planting of tough young trees and shrubs which will eventually supersede the fencing as they spread closer together and attain height.

Inside the garden tall-growing plants benefit from being arranged in groups for mutual support and protection – triangular formations offer maximum stability – and these groups in their turn afford protection for the smaller plants you grow around them. If you want quick results it is better to use young plants generously than to risk losing mature container-grown specimens which will be more prone to stress in new surroundings. Dense planting compensates visually for slow initial growth and any casualties on the way will be a little less obvious and a lot less heart-breaking.

Seaside gardening is no holiday. By the sea the physical drying effect of the wind is often compounded by a chemical one. Squalls carry sea spray inland and deposit salt on leaves and stems. This draws moisture out of them by a process known as osmosis, and can lead to scorching. Salt water in soil can have a similarly detrimental effect on roots, which can lead, perversely, to symptoms of drought after a heavy sea storm. If you've ever seen the aftermath of prolonged flooding in seafront gardens you can finally stop puzzling over why things looked more burnt than rotten: 'Water, water, everywhere, / Nor any drop to drink.' As if salt weren't enough to contend with, when sand is whipped up too it has a harsh abrasive effect which can kill off young plants, wipe out new growth on established ones, and cause long-term scarring and deformation on older woody stems. Sandstorms can even bury low-growing and ground-cover plants!

All this sounds alarming, and it is unfortunately true that a harsh winter will come round now and again to set back or destroy many healthy plants that have been growing for years, but it's not all bad news. As well as taking every possible step to protect your garden and keep damage to a minimum – as for any windy garden – the hard work spent defying salt- and sand-laden gales will be amply repaid if you progressively exploit the planting opportunities offered by a coastal location.

Snow rarely falls around the coast, and it thaws quickly if it settles as salt is a natural antifreeze. The briny air also discourages frost formation and this extends the life-expectancy of tender plants, often enabling them to grow for several years instead of needing to be treated as annuals, and dramatically increases the range of shrubs, climbers and perennials which can be relied upon to be fully hardy. Coastal soil often has a high sand

'Oh, I do like to be beside the seaside, I do like to be beside the sea . . .' Mediterranean plantings are suited to more coastal gardens than you might at first imagine.

content which makes it warm, well-aerated and free-draining, further protecting plants from cold and winter wet and getting them off to a good start in springtime.

Because salt inhibits water uptake and because plants lose moisture quickly under coastal conditions, seaside gardens, despite the high rainfall, are excellent hosts for drought-adapted plants such as stylish Mediterranean imports and even palm trees. This is why seaside resorts are always more exotic than inland towns – it's down to Mother Nature, not the carnival atmosphere. So if you're a seaside gardener who pessimistically skipped the dry gardens section, flick back and catch up on some likely plant characteristics of drought-adapted plants.

Plant features which help keep in moisture also help keep salt away – the hairs of grey- and silver-foliaged plants keep it away from the leaf surface while tough, glossy and gummy finishes prevent it from being absorbed. The golden cane palm (*Chrysalidocarpus lutescens*), which can be grown as a specimen tree in favoured locations, has the astonishing ability to get rid of salt by channelling it into selected branches which wither and die when saturated. Shrubs capable of withstanding fierce wind such as tamarisk and sea buckthorn tend to have flexible whippy stems and small leaves which offer little wind resistance; the broom family has more or less dispensed with leaves as we know them altogether. Long deep roots are excellent for anchorage and for finding water, while tough and fibrous roots such as those of *Rosa rugosa*, bladder senna (*Colutea arborescens*) and lyme grass (*Leymus arenarius*) can survive on almost pure sand, stabilizing soil and helping to counteract erosion.

Beyond successfully building a collection of plants that will survive and prosper year on year, the ultimate benefit of selecting only plants well adapted to prevailing coastal conditions is that in their struggle to grow their natural characteristics become more pronounced. Canny seasiders will waste none of their time on plants whose lives would always be balancing on a knife-edge and will have gardens bursting with far more striking specimens than those grown soft and lank in the richer soil and more sheltered location of an inland garden. Survivalists like euphorbias and eryngiums are tougher and brighter; decorative grasses like *Stipa gigantea* and *Festuca glauca* are more wiry and glaucous; gummy shrubs like myrtles and rock roses are more pungently aromatic; evergreen shrubs like hebes and olearias grow more dense and shapely in tough conditions.

When disaster strikes and you suffer a heavy salt gale there is one other step you can take to keep damage to a minimum. It is a dark and irresponsible secret never to be repeated in front of a water board official, but hosing foliage down thoroughly after a storm has saved many a fine plant from ruin. Shhh!

Damp gardens

Only a lunatic would build a house in a bog, so no one is likely to have a garden that is entirely sodden. Any sane property developer will aim to build on the highest and driest ground available. Since water always gravitates to the lowest possible level, if you do have a damp spot at all it will invariably be the furthest from the house and probably in a hollow or at the front of an incline. Unfortunately, gardeners usually follow the path of least resistance, so a damp spot is often the last area to be tackled or, 'out of sight, out of mind', it is simply ignored and forgotten. This is a shame.

Far from being a problem, a naturally occurring damp patch is a boon, and deserves to be made into a prominent feature or even the main focal point of any garden. (An unnatural damp patch is another thing altogether. In older urban properties wet ground can indicate seepage

from damaged drains or water mains and for the sake of your house you might want to get this checked out before gardening merrily on your way.)

Some of the most spectacular plants of all are those which thrive in permanently damp conditions. Their leaves can grow to enormous proportions safe in the knowledge that drought will never be a threat, and astute gardeners can double their impact by growing them beside a pool of calm reflecting water. Gardening with giants can be thrilling once you get over your early timidity, and once their impact really hits you we guarantee you'll be far more adventurous with plants for ever after. *Gunnera manicata* is the most awesome of these plants, growing like raggedy mutant rhubarb with 2m/7ft diameter leaves on 2.5m/8ft high stalks. Don't dismiss this out of hand. You don't need a country estate to enjoy it and if you've got the right conditions in a small garden one massively overscaled plant can be far more impressive than even the choicest range of tiddlers. If a gunnera really is out of the question, a few specimens of other larger-than-average plants will help draw the eye and provide maximum contrast with the rest of your garden. Skunk cabbage (*Lysichiton camtschatcensis*) is an enormous white arum lily from North East Asia with 60cm/24in flowers and 1m/3½ft leaves; its yellow-flowered cousin *L. americanus* is bigger and brasher – we make no comment. *Petasites japonicus* is a giant member of the coltsfoot family with elegant kidney-shaped leaves which are white and woolly on the underside. Rodgersias have distinctive leaves, not unlike the horse chestnut, which colour well in the autumn, and they produce tall summer plumes of cream

previous page Roses, lady's mantle and a glaucous blue euphorbia sunbathe on the banks while moisture-loving ferns, primulas and irises paddle in the shallows. One setting, so many different plant habitats.

or pink flowers. An impressive vertical accent can be provided by the giant reed *Arundo donax*, which also has several slightly less vigorous but infinitely more dramatic variegated forms – stems can attain a height of 5m/16ft in a good year.

Take one look along a riverbank and you'll see how willows adore most soils. Beware though! They are large trees and their far-reaching roots are a real menace to the foundations of buildings. Plant them only in the largest of gardens and even then with caution.

In lieu of a tree there are two shrubs we recommend unreservedly for really wet patches. Common elder rarely earns a second glance in the hedgerow but the cultivated forms of *Sambucus* all make stunning additions to any garden. Ornamental varieties range from giant-leaved specimens with the colour of eucalyptus, through standard-sized ones with leaves a handsome purple or with strong green and cream variegation, to buttercup-yellow ones with finely cut, almost fern-like foliage. They come with the added lure of milk-white or pink summer flowers and claret-coloured autumn berries. The other star shrub for Davy Jones's locker is the guelder rose (*Viburnum opulus*), which has pretty leaves not unlike a maple, pure white flowers and bunches of glistening berries in scarlet or yellow according to variety. The flowers usually resemble lace-cap hydrangeas, but those of *V.o.* 'Roseum' are show-stopping white snowballs. The one failing of 'Roseum', as its former name 'Sterile' suggests, is a complete and utter lack of berries.

Apart from such stunners as these, smaller more 'normal' plants are a piece of cake, as long as you choose damp-adapted plants. Just follow the usual advice of looking to Nature, spying on your neighbours, checking the labels in garden centres or (heaven forbid) looking things up in a book. Of course, you know better by now than to stick just anything in and imagine it'll be grateful for an extra drink.

The secret's in the soil

Dig for victory!
Feed and condition your garden with compost,
manure and the odd home remedy.
Decode the mysterious NPK.
Whether it is humus-rich or nutrient-starved,
acid or alkaline, sand, clay, peat or poorest chalk,
what soil needs most is TLC.

'Whatsoever a man soweth, that shall he also reap.' Cultivating a garden is like cultivating a friendship: the more you put in over the years the more you get back in return. A familiarity develops which helps you understand the garden's needs, and the garden in turn responds.

As far as the location and climate of your garden are concerned, the only way to effect a change is to up sticks and move house. We've already shown you how to make the most of any given conditions, so assuming you're staying put for a while we now want to get right to the heart of any successful garden. It's the soil. And once you understand how plants and soil interact you can revitalize and improve the growing conditions in any garden almost beyond your wildest expectations. Cultivating the soil enables every plant to attain its full potential.

Most soils have been created by the erosion of rocks over millions of years and are essentially mineral formations. Additional bulk has been added over the centuries by decomposed plant matter, animal dung and the bodies of animals themselves. The generic term for this organic material is humus. It improves soil texture, holding on to moisture and so retaining nutrients in solution which can then be absorbed by roots as and when plants require them. Healthy soil is also teeming with micro-organisms including algae, bacteria and fungi and all kinds of mini-beasts such as insects, spiders and worms.

Everybody's soil is different, and the quality of soil can vary enormously even within a single garden. Growing conditions are affected by the structure and balance of all these individual constituents, by the depth of the soil, and by its water content. Once you realize that soil is

previous page Azaleas and rhododendrons thrive in acid soil. Plant them in poor, dry, chalky soil, and they'll be as skinny as shilling rabbits.

something far greater than the sum of its parts you develop a more holistic approach to gardening which makes life far less frustrating and a little bit more rewarding. Before floating off into soil nirvana though, it's time to get down and dirty.

Types of soil

Broadly speaking, soil falls into five different categories.

Sand

The difference between light and heavy soils is mostly due to particle size. Sandy soils, with their granular structure, are easy to dig because they're well aerated and very free draining. In sandy soil roots can breathe and are unlikely to rot or suffer frost damage over winter because they're not sitting in water. Sandy soil is quick to warm up in spring, so plants get off with a flying start to the year. However, because sandy soils lose moisture rapidly, plants growing in them are prone to drought in summer and a

A

B

C

D

It's easier than you think to suss out your soil. These four piles of earth represent sand, clay, loam and chalk. Which is which?

A loam
B sand
C clay
D chalk

related problem is that soluble plant foods are quickly washed through the soil in the wetter months of the year. Like all light soils, sand benefits from heavy applications of organic matter to aid water-retention and to replenish nutrients. Autumn cultivation makes drainage even more rapid and leads to increased leaching of plant foods, so to get the maximum benefit from compost and manure it is best to dig it in after the winter weather has done its worst.

Clay

Because clay particles are so fine they stick very closely together when wet to give a heavy soil which is hard to cultivate. Digging it wet can compound the problems of waterlogging and poor aeration. Digging it dry can be near impossible: it sets like concrete. To keep the existing soil structure as open as possible it is a good idea when working in the vegetable patch to stand on boards to distribute your weight over a wider area. If you lay the occasional small paving slab inside the flower border you can create a network of stepping stones to give easy access to plants without unduly compacting the soil with your feet.

The addition of bulky organic material helps open up the texture, and coarse grit and sand improve drainage. Autumn cultivation works best but you have to wait for one of the rare occasions when the soil is neither too dry and hard nor too wet and sticky. Clay soil should be dug with the backbone of a navvy but the light touch of a pastry chef; prolonged effort or too heavy a hand and the end result is dense and leaden. A useful tip is to leave the surface as loose and rough as possible; this allows frost to

Like so many other wildflowers, the oxeye daisy (*Leucanthemum vulgare*) prefers a frugal diet. Chalk and sandy soil suit it admirably.

penetrate over winter and to break up large compacted clods. Unfortunately, a major problem can arise with clay soil in the summer, from a prolonged absence of rain combined with baking heat from the sun. Clay shrinks as it dries out, producing splits and cracks on the surface which not only give the soil a far greater surface area, thus accelerating the drying process, but also lead to root damage.

However, if you have a clay soil, do not despair. Clay is actually a very desirable soil. Although a nuisance in winter, its water-retaining qualities can be a blessing in summer, as it is far more drought-resistant than sand and can play host to a far wider range of plants. Because it is formed from rock dissolved over millions of years by mild acid erosion, rather than by geological activity or weathering by the elements, it has a high content of mineral salts and has the potential to be very fertile indeed.

Loam

Somewhere between the two extremes of sand and clay, loam is a combination of large and small particles. It is lighter, warmer and easier to work than clay and retains more moisture and nutrients than sand. Once enriched with sufficient humus, loam is the best possible garden soil.

Loams vary widely in texture according to the relative proportions of clay, sand and humus in their make-up, and these will affect how they can best be cultivated. A heavy clay loam will benefit from an autumn dig incorporating compost or manure and possibly some sand or grit. A light sandy loam will respond best to lashings of humus in spring, your aim being to make it like Little Bear's porridge – just right.

Peat

Peat soils are organic rather than mineral in content, composed of many, many years' worth of fully decomposed plant matter. The words 'peat' and 'bog' go hand in hand for a very good reason: with its spongy texture, peat is always prone to waterlogging. This tendency can be alleviated to some extent by digging in coarse grit and sand to open up the soil texture. Peat is a soft and welcoming medium for plant roots, so any manuring and fertilizing is done more to enrich the soil with nutrients than to improve its texture or increase its water-retaining properties.

Chalk

People worry, quite unnecessarily, that they won't be able to grow anything at all on chalk soil simply because it contains lime and they've heard a few rumbles and murmurs about lime-hating plants. Fear not! Chalk soil suits such a wide variety of plants that even if you can't grow ericas, azaleas or rhododendrons there'll be plenty of substitutes to choose from.

Any setbacks involved in gardening on chalk are more to do with soil structure than chemistry. Because they are generally shallow, stony and free draining, chalk soils are quick to lose water and nutrients. Pale, dry and hungry-looking, they benefit more from a good feed than any other type of soil. The water-retaining qualities can be improved by digging in copious amounts of organic matter and by mulching generously. As you dig in organic matter over the years you can actually see the topsoil becoming darker and richer. Vegetables adore a well-cultivated chalk soil above all else, and members of the cabbage family positively thrive, since lime helps keep their arch enemy, club root, at bay.

Soil pH

Soil pH is a major cause of paranoia. Virgin gardeners are always worried that ignorance will affect their technique and show up in poor performance. When put on the spot, older gardeners who've been happy for years are suddenly as embarrassed as if they've forgotten the names of all their children. It never seems to occur to people that their soil is probably just right, and that they should never allow themselves to be intimidated by science babble.

Soil chemistry is a fascinating subject, and from the gardener's point of view it is perfectly straightforward. Soils are made up of a wide variety of natural materials and will be alkaline if largely composed of chalk or limestone, and acid if full of peat and humus.

Rainfall leaches lime away. Decomposing leaf matter is always present and is acid-forming. It follows that the average garden is slightly acid.

Some plants are better adapted to a more acid soil, others prefer a slightly alkaline one; most are quite happy with whatever is on offer. The few that mind very much indeed are the ones which set everyone panicking. Don't panic – just treat them like fussy eaters at a dinner party. If you like them very much indeed and you're prepared to cater specially for them, do so by all means. If you can't be fagged, you can always enjoy their

company elsewhere. If acid lovers such as rhododendrons, azaleas and heathers are an absolute must but your garden soil is alkaline, you can grow them in containers or a raised bed of imported peaty soil. To increase the fertility of an acid vegetable patch you can add lime.

Helping Nature along is one thing; tampering is quite another. Some shrubs suffer from nutrient deficiencies on alkaline soil and can be kept going with regular doses of sequestered iron, but is it really worth it when there are plenty of other plants to choose from? You can use ammonium sulphate to turn pink hydrangeas blue, but what's the point? You are the host, your plants are the guests and the aim is for everyone to be happy and relaxed without, we hope, any dependency on artificial stimulants.

The pH scale, the gardener and the businessman

• The pH scale measures acidity and alkalinity running from extremely acid at 0, through to neutral at 7, then up to 14 for extremely alkaline.

• The optimum pH for most plants is 6.5, which is slightly acid, but natural soil pH can be anywhere between 5 and 7.5.

• Vegetables generally prefer a neutral soil, so lime is often added to acid soil to raise the pH. This is quite traditional and generally beneficial.

• Soil-testing kits are widely available and usually recommend corrective treatment for your soil based on the results they give. The companies who sell the kits helpfully sell the products they recommend for the treatment.

• Science is a marvellous thing, but few people leave an opticians without a pair of glasses. If you don't think you've got a problem, don't go looking for one.

Improving the soil

You only have to dig a deep hole to realize that soil is built up in layers and to see that the most important one for the gardener is the top layer or topsoil, which provides plants with an anchor and acts as a larder of nutrients. The richer and deeper it is, the healthier your plants are. This is where you and your spade come in.

Even without adding organic matter, lightly turning over the soil can help aerate and revivify it in preparation for planting. However, nothing can beat a thorough and systematic digging which simultaneously incorporates a generous amount of humus. Investing in healthy soil gives huge dividends in fruit, vegetable and flower production and acts as insurance against pests and diseases. It really is worth the little trouble it takes, and if you work rhythmically and in easy stages it's good exercise not hard labour. It's a once-only job when preparing a flower bed, and only a quarter of your vegetable plot needs doing each year if you operate a crop rotation system.

Single digging

Working along a plot a row at a time, simply turn over the soil to the depth of a spade incorporating muck – organic material – as you go. This sounds easy enough but in practice it can be quite laborious unless you know a simple trick. All you have to do is to remove the soil from the first trench entirely and lay it to one side. Then as you dig along the next row the soil neatly turns over and more or less falls into the adjacent trench

Dead plant matter is drawn into the soil by burrowing earthworms and broken down further by micro-organisms into soluble plant nutrients which can be absorbed by roots for the cycle to begin again. This is Nature's way of aerating soil and improving its texture and nutrient value. As gardeners we make heavy demands on our soil and must dig, condition and fertilize to compensate.

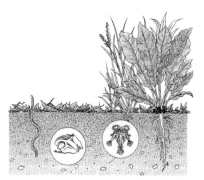

with minimal help from you. The soil from the next row then fills the trench you have just created, and so on. By using a bit of brain you get gravity to do half your work.

Now for some advanced technique. The top inch or so of soil usually holds a large number of weed seeds and may also be home to the eggs and larvae of troublesome insects. Skimming off the surface layer of soil and dumping it into the bottom of the trench before you turn over the greater bulk of soil on top of it significantly reduces the need for weeding later in the year and can help break the life cycle of persistent pests.

The most efficient way to incorporate organic material is to spread it along the top of each row once you've skimmed off the surface layer. It is then incorporated into the top spit of soil as you (and your good friend gravity) turn it over shovelful by shovelful into the trench.

Those among you of a reflective nature might be wondering by now about that first trenchful of soil. Glad you asked. As you dig over the last row you'll be left with an empty trench. That's where you put it! Diagrams in old gardening books make a big meal of this, invariably showing heavy wheelbarrows of soil being carted from one end of a plot to the other. If you're mad or if you're a bodybuilder, do this by all means. Otherwise, use a spot of creative visualization and you need barely lift a finger. Let's assume you're working backwards row by row down the length of your plot. Now divide the plot lengthwise down the middle. As you take out the first spadeful of soil from the corner of your plot, dump it outside the plot but near this imaginary middle line. As you work along the row, dump each new shovelful next to the previous one. When you've dug out a

By caring sensibly for your soil you subtly tip the balance of Nature in your favour to create a happy, healthy home for your flowers. Idly spoonfeeding with chemicals does nothing for the earth and gives you plants like fat soulless mummy's boys.

trench to the middle, stop. The trench you've got enables you to dig the full length of your plot but in short rows which are half its width. You then fill in the trench at the bottom of the plot with soil you dig out from the other half of that row. Lo and behold! You can now dig in the opposite direction up the remaining half of your plot, and the final trench is filled in with the soil you dug out at the very beginning. And not a wheelbarrow in sight!

Double digging

Single digging gives your garden a good seeing to but double digging is on a par with Tantric sex. It doesn't mean digging your garden over twice. It involves cultivating the soil to a depth of two spits, keeping the fertile topsoil on the surface and incorporating muck as in single digging, but also forking and conditioning the subsoil as you go. With regular double digging the subsoil eventually attains the quality of topsoil, giving you deeper and richer beds which are of especial benefit in growing potatoes and other root vegetable crops. Here goes. Dig out a trench. Fork over the soil in the base of the trench, incorporating organic matter as you work. Turn over the topsoil from the next row as in single digging, also incorporating organic matter. Then fork over the newly revealed subsoil as

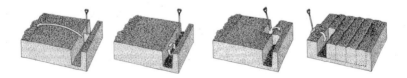

Bewildering at first, the logistics of double digging are easily grasped with spade in hand. It's a deeply satisfying process and soon becomes an addiction. As you warm to the theme you'll come up with countless variations of your own.

above and continue along the plot.

There are countless variations on double digging, the most useful being a technique for digging up old lawns or very weedy soil. Dig out a trench one spit deep. Incorporate the turf or weeds from the next row into the bottom of the second spit. Turn over the remaining topsoil and incorporate organic matter as for single digging. And on and on and on. At the end of the process you will have buried your weeds or your entire lawn two spades deep where they will rot down nicely to improve the subsoil, and you'll have cultivated the topsoil ready for planting. Phew! If you ever need to do this on a really large scale and you're mathematically minded, you might consider the possibilities offered by removing two rows of topsoil and one row of subsoil before you begin . . .

So much for the digging. But what, precisely, should you dig in? If you're ecologically minded, avoid peat. This has been sold as a soil improver for years, but it carries the hidden cost of destroying wildlife habitats in the countryside. And as you already know, its nutrient content is low. Better, sustainable alternatives are compost and manure. Spent hops, seaweed, wool shoddy and old mushroom compost can all be used to improve soil texture too, but their nutrient content is lower and less well-balanced than that of either compost or manure.

Compost

One name, two completely different animals. Potting compost is a peat- or loam-based medium used as a soil substitute. Garden compost is a dark and aromatic compote made of well-rotted garden and kitchen waste and any other organic material you can lay your hands on. Too rich by itself, it is used to condition soil and improve fertility.

There is a huge mystique about making garden compost, and it's high time it was dispelled. For one thing you don't need a huge elaborate container. Piling the stuff up on the ground works just fine. If it blows around a bit you can cover the heap with sacking or old blankets. These keep everything in place while allowing the compost to breathe. Making fancy boxes is a displacement activity for latent DIY enthusiasts. You will never need anything more elaborate than four posts and some chicken wire. If you've ever so much as contemplated making a compost bin in the form of a wooden beehive with a lift-off lid we suggest your talents would be better deployed indoors perfecting elaborate paint techniques and putting up la-di-da dado rails.

Anything that rots down can be put on the heap. But there are a few provisos. Woody prunings hang around for ever so are best excluded or burnt and added in the form of wood ash. Diseased plant material can cause contamination so is better binned or burnt. Large compost heaps generate a lot of heat at the core but this can't be relied upon to kill viruses or fungal spores. At the end of a year leave your heap alone and start another one. The first heap will be ready when it's ready – it is impossible to give guidelines as your climate, the size of the heap, its composition and its moisture content will all affect the rate of decomposition. Just fork it over occasionally to improve its texture and when its consistency has been uniform for some time it has probably rotted as much as it's going to and you might as well use it.

Some people add soil to their heaps, but this is a waste of time. There are quite enough bacteria-laden soil particles on the garden waste you add to speed up decomposition. Others, heaven forbid, add chemical accelerators. What's the rush? There's only one compost accelerator we recommend. Encourage the men in your household to pee on the heap whenever the opportunity arises. Besides keeping the compost moist, urine adds valuable nitrates. Ladies' contributions are of course equally welcome but harder to deliver with equanimity.

Gardening is about give and take. It's like the courtesy of return entertaining. Let your potato plot gorge on a rich diet of compost and manure and it'll be offering you dinner in no time.

Manure

A panacea for all evils, good manure improves the texture of light and heavy soils alike and is a complete plant food in itself.

What is generally known as manure consists largely of cow manure mixed up with straw litter. It might also have some horse and pig manure thrown in. Horse manure is often to be had for the asking from racing stables and riding schools in the country and from police stables in towns and cities. Horses are generally kept in greater comfort than cows, so the litter content is higher than for farmyard manure. If cow and horse manure are Cheddar and Cheshire, pig manure is ripe Brie. Although an excellent source of nutrients it is smelly, runny and hard to handle. Not to everyone's taste!

Neat poultry manure is a rich source of nutrients but as these leach out quickly it is best consigned to the compost heap. Considering the disgusting conditions in most battery units you might prefer to check where it comes from before using it.

Whatever kind of manure you use it should be well rotted down before you dig it in. Otherwise nitrogen is temporarily diverted from the soil to aid decomposition and although plants gain in the long term they lose out in the short term. If you have the opportunity to collect your manure yourself always try to dig from the middle of the muck heap. That way you get really rich and well-rotted stuff that can be used straightaway instead of being composted for a year first.

Plant nutrients

You might recall that we began this book by discussing photosynthesis, the process by which all green plants manufacture food. In which case you may be wondering what this talk of plant nutrients is about.

Oxygen, carbon and hydrogen from the air and from water account for a staggering 96 per cent of a plant's nutrient requirements. But 4 per cent has to be supplied from the soil. Nitrogen and potassium account for 1.5 per cent each, phosphorus just 0.15 per cent. After these three essential elements, plants need 0.5 per cent calcium, 0.2 per cent magnesium, 0.1 per cent sulphur and infinitesimal traces of boron, copper, iron, manganese and zinc.

Nitrogen (N)

A component of chlorophyll and a major constituent of plant proteins, nitrogen is responsible for green growth – increasing the length of stems and the size of leaves. Nitrogen deficiency shows in yellow leaves and stunted growth. Too much nitrogen leads to soft sappy growth which is prone to attack from insects and less able to stand up to frost.

Phosphorus (P)

Although this is the second most important element for plants after nitrogen, they only need one tenth the amount of it compared to either nitrogen or potassium. It is mainly responsible for the growth and maintenance of roots but also helps counterbalance the effects on a plant's metabolism of nitrogen. A deficiency will show in under-developed roots leading to less vigorous and even stunted top-growth.

Potassium (K)

Usually referred to as potash by gardeners, it encourages the healthy growth of flowers and fruit, affecting both size and quality. Potash is the element missing from many organic fertilizers. Rock potash helps correct any shortcomings and a liquid feed made from comfrey leaves can give a quick boost. Tomatoes are particularly hungry for potash.

General fertilizers

Should you wish to boost soil fertility, you can do so by applying N, P and K in any of a number of forms, as you condition the soil and at the beginning of the growing season. Be sure to follow the instructions on any proprietary products. For long-term benefit though, nothing really beats enriching the soil by digging in organic matter.

Many natural fertilizers contain N, P and K in combination. Manure is the prime example, with one ton of the stuff holding 4.5kg N, 4.5kg K and 2.25kg P. More concentrated slow-releasing organic fertilizers include seaweed meal and blood, fish and bone. Seaweed extract is an excellent all-round tonic and can be applied as a foliar feed for fast results. Because these are natural products the nutrient value can vary from batch to batch, but natural gardening is not a precise science and this is nothing to worry about. Mineral or synthetic fertilizers on the other hand should be used advisedly and with caution. Like any fertilizers these work best in soil with a high humus or clay content because they can be held in solution around plant roots. Unlike slower-acting natural fertilizers they can produce such a quick burst of growth that gardeners look on them as wonder drugs and neglect to cultivate their soil. As the humus content of the soil depletes, fertilizers are leached away ever more quickly, and higher and more frequent dosages are required. Farmers have been reliant on artificial fertilizers for years and soil structure on arable land has deteriorated so significantly that fertilizer run-off and the subsequent

'Yes, here is the mine of gold and silver, gold medals and silver cups for the grower of prize Roses; and to all who love them, the best diet for their health and beauty, the most strengthening tonic for their weakness, and the surest medicine for disease.' – Dean Hole, extolling the virtues of poultry manure in *A Book About Roses*, 1869.

pollution of rivers and water courses has become commonplace. Aside from this kind of damage it is worth remembering that too high a concentration of one chemical can inhibit the uptake of another. For example, with too much potassium in the soil plants can't absorb sufficient magnesium.

Once you start using chemicals to tinker with Nature in your garden you are standing at the top of a very slippery slope. There is a real danger that in counterbalancing one deficiency you will simply set up another. Counteracting that one will lead to another. And so on.

Nitrogenous fertilizers

- *Dried blood* – this is fast-acting and good for a quick nitrogen boost.
- *Fish meal* – this also contains phosphates. Some manufacturers add potassium to create an all-purpose plant food.
- *Hoof and horn* – this is an excellent slow-release nitrogen fertilizer.
- *Soot* – this also raises soil temperature by darkening its colour and increasing its capacity to absorb heat.
- *Wool shoddy* – a by-product of the wool industry, this acts as a slow-release fertilizer as well as a soil conditioner.
- *Sulphate of ammonia.*
- *Nitrate of soda.*

Phosphatic fertilizers

- *Bonemeal* – to avoid health hazards always wear gloves during use.
- *Basic slag* – an iron industry by-product. It is dirty but efficient.
- *Fish meal* – primarily a nitrogenous fertilizer, this also contains some phosphates.
- *Superphosphate of lime* – sulphuric acid is used in the manufacturing process. How nice!

Potash fertilizers

- *Rock potash* – it is interesting to note that being a mineral this is perfectly natural but not organic. On the other hand, manure from battery-reared animals fed and injected with God alone knows what may be organic in origin but is far from natural.
- *Wood ash* – while all wood ash is valuable as a soil improver, the ash from young wood and from shrub prunings has a higher potassium content than ash from old wood.
- *Extract of comfrey leaves* – see below.
- *Potassium nitrate* – also known as nitrate of potash but best known as saltpetre. Excellent in fireworks.

Comfrey extract

To make a fast-acting – and free – liquid fertilizer, pack a plastic bucket with comfrey leaves then fill it with water to cover. Russian comfrey (*Symphytum × uplandicum*) is usually used but, if you can get it, the variety 'Bocking 14' contains twice as much potassium. Leave it to steep for several weeks then apply the strained liquid diluted in about twelve parts water. Consign what remains of the leaves to the compost heap. Waste not, want not.

Food from your garden

*Know your onions and
kitchen gardening couldn't be simpler.
Grow your vegetables according to
their plant families and you'll find
you have only four cultivation groups to deal with.
Move them round each year
and you're a master of crop rotation.
The ground rules for herbs and fruit trees
are more straightforward still.*

Vegetables

Growing your own vegetables is an amazing experience. The process is almost magical. In the course of a few months, or sometimes even a few short weeks, seeds from a packet or young plants from a nursery are transformed into food for your plate.

Because you are taking a lot out of the ground it is important that you put a lot back in. But just as cookery books can be rather irritating when they repeatedly tell you to take a clean bowl or to put something in a clean saucepan – are they implying that you normally use dirty ones? – gardening books too impugn your character by telling you a thousand times to plant things in well-prepared ground. You know the benefits; the choice is yours. We will simply fill you in on the cultivation techniques different plants require to perform really well.

Plants cultivated as vegetables fall into distinct family groups, which can be a helpful indicator of the growing conditions they prefer.

Potato family (*Solanaceae*)

One of the most important vegetables to mankind, potatoes have been in cultivation since pre-Columbian times. The Irish famine of 1846 occurred when the entire country was stricken with potato blight. Tomatoes, peppers, aubergines and tobacco are also members of this family.

Carrot family (*Apiaceae/Umbelliferae*)

Easily recognized in bloom by their characteristic flat flower heads, some members of this family are otherwise rather well disguised. The fleshy

previous page As attractive as it is useful, ruby-stemmed chard runs spectacularly to seed in its second season. Leave a few plants to bolt just for the joy of it.

roots of carrots and parsnips are easy to spot of course, but celery and fennel are close relatives grown for their stalks, parsley is grown for its leaves, and celeriac is grown for its swollen stem base.

Onion family (*Alliaceae*)

Onions, shallots and garlic are grown primarily for their bulbs, while leeks and chives are grown for their leaves. As long as they don't have any problems with pests or diseases, onions can be grown in the same place for many years.

Lettuce family (*Asteraceae/Compositae*)

These are all related to daisies. Yes, really! If you want to check out the relationship, just compare lettuce, chicory, endive, salsify and scorzonera with a daisy on your lawn. The sap and roots have a characteristic smell, and the flowers are a dead giveaway.

Beetroot family (*Chenopodiaceae*)

It's easy to think of spinach and cabbage as similar, both being 'greens', but the minute you think about it, it's obvious that spinach has nothing to do with cabbage. Beetroot, sugar beet, chard, orach, spinach and spinach beet are all variations on a theme.

Cucumber family (*Cucurbitaceae*)

This family includes cucumbers, courgettes, marrows, squashes and pumpkins. Some of these plants are technically fruits, but they're vegetables from a practical point of view. Children, bores and botanists love to nit-pick but if an argument starts developing, the rest of us can just apply the custard test. If you can't serve it with custard it's a vegetable. QED.

Brassica family (*Brassicaceae/Cruciferae*)

Many of these are grown for their leaves, cabbages, kale and Brussels sprouts being the obvious examples. Broccoli, calabrese and cauliflower are grown primarily for their flower buds and stems. Radishes, swedes and turnips are grown for their fat, swollen roots. All brassicas have the distinctive 'cabbagey' smell and all parts of the plants are edible: cooked cauliflower greens and turnip tops are just as delicious as pickled radish seed pods. Although rape is usually grown for the oil in its seeds, young plants can be used as a mustard and cress substitute.

Pea family (*Papilionaceae/Leguminosae*)

Leguminous plants are a tough and enterprising lot. Peas and beans have a symbiotic relationship with certain nitrogen-fixing bacteria in the soil. They obtain nitrogen from these bacteria in exchange for carbohydrates, the process taking place in nodules on their roots. After you have cropped the plants and consigned the top-growth to the compost heap, the plant roots should be worked thoroughly into the soil to enrich it with nitrogen.

Crop rotation

Given that similar plants enjoy similar conditions, it is common sense to grow related vegetables in the same patch. You can also cut out a lot of fuss and bother when you realize that the cultivation requirements of many quite different vegetables are in fact the same. There are four broad groups of vegetable families to consider. If you divide your plot into quarters and grow each group of related vegetables together, you'll have a full choice every season, and with minimum weekly maintenance.

Orderly vegetable beds bounded by simple pathways make crop rotation a simple and straightforward practice rather than a memory feat for a music-hall turn.

Crop rotation

1 Potato family

Potatoes are a class apart. They are heavy feeders and they deplete soil rapidly, preferring deep muck-rich beds and rather more acidic conditions than other root vegetables. They are also prone to disease if grown in the same place for too long.

2 Carrot, onion, lettuce, beetroot and cucumber families

Carrots, onions, lettuces, beetroots and cucumbers aren't quite such greedy feeders and they prefer a rather more alkaline soil. Before planting them after clearing a potato bed you can add a little ground lime or calcified seaweed, give it a light dig and your work is done. Carrots like rich soil, although too rich a soil encourages onion bulbs to rot.

3 Brassica family

If brassicas are grown in the same ground year upon year they attract a very wide range of insect pests such as cabbage root fly, cabbage white fly and cabbage white butterflies. To prevent the pests, their eggs or their larvae from building up in force a cunning move is to plant them in fresh ground each year. Their nutrient requirements are adequately met by soil which has previously grown vegetables like carrots and onions. Brassicas are happiest in soil that is well firmed at planting time so don't dig it too vigorously.

4 Pea family

Because peas and beans add so much nitrogen to the soil it is a good idea to grow them after vegetables like cabbages whose heavy green growth depletes nitrogen reserves. You might think you could grow the most enormous cabbages in the world if you planted them after peas and beans. Think again. Too much nitrogen encourages fast growth and long stems so they tend not to heart properly and may quickly run to seed. Peas and beans appreciate single digging with the addition of muck a month or so before sowing. Tired soil that has produced crops continuously for four years deserves a treat. Double digging old pea and bean beds with a good dose of muck conditions the soil, replenishes nitrogen reserves and boosts fertility with a balanced dose of N, P and K in one fell swoop. This makes the soil just right for potatoes. Again.

If at the end of the year you move your groups of crops around from patch to patch so that they follow each other in the sequence described opposite, you also keep annual soil preparation down, fertility up, pests and diseases down and productivity up. You just can't lose.

Before proceeding any further you should congratulate yourself on your understanding of crop rotation.

Rules are made to be broken, so don't get worked up about all this. Every little helps so just do what you can. The main thing is to keep things moving, as the actress said to the bishop.

In view of all this information it is interesting to see how the traditional design of an ornamental kitchen garden or potager developed. Allowing for fruit trees and for permanent plantings of vegetables such as asparagus, cardoons and artichokes, the archetype is a square plot cut into four by two crossing paths. Absolutely perfect for crop rotation and a classic case of form following function!

We'll now look at a few selected vegetables in detail. For all vegetables though, just remember that the best guide to growing is the back of the seed packet. Seed companies want healthy crops and happy customers. Put your faith in them.

Potatoes

These are divided into three groups: early, mid-season and late. The names reflect the length of time they take to reach maturity as much as the season to harvest. An 'early' variety planted late will mature long before a 'late' variety planted early. To get them off to a flying start, 'seed' potatoes can be chitted – left in a light airy place to sprout shoots up to 3cm/1in long – before being planted out in mid- to late spring after frost is no longer a danger. Any weak shoots should be rubbed away with your fingers before planting the 'seed' so that the shoots, whether vertical or horizontal, are 10cm/4in below soil level. Early varieties, which mature younger and smaller than mid-seasons and lates, can be grown closer together but a good general planting distance is 45cm/18in.

When the potato plants are about 15cm/6in high, ridge up the earth around them with a hoe to cover the developing tubers and to protect the hollow stems from wind damage. Late varieties will benefit from a second earthing up later in the season. Earlies will be ready for harvest by early summer, mid-seasons by mid-summer and lates by early to mid-autumn. Unless you've got X-ray eyes the only sure way to tell if they're ready is to poke away gently at the ridges with your bare hands and see what you find. If you still can't decide, try rubbing the skin with your fingers. If it can't be easily rubbed off, you can put the saucepan on. If it quickly comes clean away, better luck next time.

Cabbages

If you've only ever eaten shop-bought greens, the taste of really fresh cabbage will come as such a revelation you'll want to eat it all year round. This is perfectly possible. Depending on variety, cabbages can be planted in autumn for harvest in spring or in spring for harvest in summer. If you plant rows thickly and eat the thinnings as the plants grow and need more space, you'll have cabbage on the table every day. Young cabbage plants can be bought from nurseries, but for once we can't recommend the easy way out as you run the risk of introducing club root, a persistent disease, into your garden. Instead, grow them from seed in pots or in a nursery bed before planting them out in rows when well grown. Careful handling and copious watering are crucial at this stage. Young plants should be firmed in well to ensure they develop a good heart. To harvest a cabbage it is wiser to cut the head off rather than pull the whole plant up and damage the roots of its neighbours. An interesting trick with spring cabbages is to take a knife and make two slits crosswise across the remaining stump. A few weeks later there'll be four baby cabbages growing there. Also smacking of witchcraft is the old wrinkle of sprinkling a teaspoon of salt

For big fat cabbages and towering spikes of sprouts, leave plenty of growing space between young brassicas when you plant them out.

around each cabbage plant in autumn to guard against winter frost. This is not just a folksy old piece of garden lore – it really works, and if you cast your mind back a chapter or so you will be able to fathom out why.

Tomatoes

If you've got a greenhouse, you can raise tomatoes by sowing three seeds to a pot in late winter or early spring then thinning to the strongest seedling after a week or two's growth. If you're not too fussy about which variety you grow, it's easier to buy pot-grown specimens at planting time in late spring. Early ripening varieties are best for growing outdoors and need a hot sunny spot, preferably against a wall, which will help them ripen by retaining heat and reflecting light. Train the plants up canes and, except in the case of bush varieties, pinch out any side shoots as they appear. Keep an eye on the flowers and when four trusses of tiny fruit have set, pinch out the growing point of the plant too. This is known as stopping, and encourages the plant to put all its energy into the tomatoes. Feeding the plant potash will stimulate fruit size, but remember that large fruits take longer to ripen. If you're not very optimistic about your summer sunshine, for God's sake hold back on the fertilizer – small ripe tomatoes are a lot more use than large green ones. Because greenhouse varieties are more pampered and cherry tomatoes have such small fruit, they can both be fed more heavily than those common or garden outdoors types and allowed to set more trusses before stopping. Tomatoes sometimes split their skins if they suddenly receive an unexpected and heavy watering after a dry spell. Guard against this by keeping the surrounding soil consistently moist.

Lettuces

Nothing could be easier to grow. Merely sow the seeds and stand back. As with cabbages, you just eat the thinnings as the plants grow. Because they mature so quickly, lettuce sowings can be made close to slower-growing crops such as carrots, onions and celery. In the brassica bed, radishes can be grown in the same way. The technique is known as catch cropping.

Onions

As well behaved as lettuces but rather slower-growing. Onions virtually lift themselves out of the ground as they mature and by harvest-time they're more or less sitting on the soil. You can help the onions ripen by bending the green tops flat to get full sun on the bulbs.

Runner beans

No vegetable plot or allotment looks quite right without rows of beans with their scarlet flowers climbing up bamboo wigwams or twining around the strings of a sturdy maypole. Gardeners are often so proud of themselves when building these features that they overlook a fundamental detail. There's no point in making them so high that you can't pick the beans at the top. Beans can be sown in pots and transplanted, but it's a lot easier to sow them *in situ*. As insurance against poor germination or rodent theft it is wise to plant two beans near each support. If two plants come up, thin out the weaker one. A late spring sowing will keep you in beans from mid-summer to the first frost; regular picking encourages more pods to form.

Herbs

The majority of useful herbs belong to just three plant families:

- *Lamiaceae/Labiatae* – balm, basil, bergamot, hyssop, lavender, marjoram, mint, oregano, pennyroyal, rosemary, sage, savory, thyme.
- *Apiaceae/Umbelliferae* – angelica, caraway, dill, fennel, lovage, parsley.
- *Asteraceae/Compositae* – chamomile, cotton lavender, marigold, southernwood, tansy, tarragon, wormwood, yarrow.

Only a few common herbs fall outside these categories. Bay, borage, chives and rue are the obvious ones. Be very careful with rue as it can be poisonous and may cause chronic skin irritation.

Plant the *Asteraceae/Compositae* anywhere and, being easy-going plants, they'll be just fine. If anything they do themselves most justice in rather poor soil – it brings out the best of their natural characteristics.

The *Apiaceae/Umbelliferae* are harder to please. With their long tap-roots they prefer a rich deep soil and they will only thrive if you find the right place for them in the garden. None of them does well in containers.

At first glance the *Lamiaceae/Labiatae* are a disparate bunch: some have rounded leaves and hug the ground in dumpy hummocks, while others are tall and distinguished with leaves like silvery pine needles. Look at them carefully and you'll see how closely related they all are with their square stems and two-lipped flowers which nestle among the leaves. Some are suited to harsher conditions than others. Balm, basil, bergamot and

We haven't all got the space to grow our own vegetables but everyone can find room for a few pots of herbs.

mint are moisture-loving; the rest are better adapted to dry sunny climes.

If you want to grow herbs in containers, simply remember not to mix moisture lovers and sun worshippers in the same pot. You can't keep both of them happy at the same time. Of all the herbs only basil, which loves the heat and protection of a warm windowsill, is suitable for cultivation indoors. With the possible exception of parsley you won't need more than one specimen of each herb, so growing from seed is wasteful unless you buy a well-mixed packet. Parsley, by the way, takes up to eight weeks to germinate, so don't hold your breath. Basil can be cropped within weeks.

Nurseries and garden centres sell herb plants in pots and this is the best way to assemble your collection. Beware the pots from supermarkets. They are crammed with seedlings which are intended for immediate culinary use. Don't waste a supermarket pot by trying to grow it on – your chances of success are virtually nil. You'd be just as mad to sacrifice a tender young seedling from the garden centre for the sake of a garnish.

Fruit

From a gardener's point of view the cultivation of fruit is frankly rather dull compared to the cut-and-thrust world of vegetable growing. Once a fruit tree or shrub is planted it more or less takes care of itself; all you have to do is remember to pick the crop.

Given the relative ease of cultivation it's surprising that fruit growing is a novelty to so many people. No garden is so small it can't accommodate an apple, a pear, a cherry or a plum. If you've got a hot sunny wall you could even try an apricot or fig tree, or perhaps a grapevine. The adventurous bit is over as soon as you've made your purchase. So why not give it a go? There's a nagging fear at the back of your mind, isn't there? They need pruning. Gentle reader, turn the page if you dare . . .

Fringed lavender
(*Lavandula
dentata*)

Spearmint (*Mentha
spicata*)

Sweet marjoram
(*Origanum majorana*)

Angelica (*Angelica
archangelica*)

French parsley
(*Petroselinum crispum
var. neapolitanum*)

Southernwood
(*Artemisia
abrotanum*)

German chamomile
(*Matricaria recutita*)

Yarrow (*Achillea
millefolium*)

Pruning

Pruning is a paradox to the uninitiated.
How can a plant grow big and strong
if some dirty great brute keeps cutting it back?
However, with the basic skills –
the how-tos, the wheres and the whens –
at your fingertips,
your shrubs, roses, climbers, hedges and trees
will flourish as never before.

The word 'pruning' strikes fear in the hearts of more gardeners than will care to admit it, yet once the underlying principles are understood the procedures involved are actually easy and straightforward. Grasp them and you'll soon be such an expert that not only will your own garden be pruned to perfection, but you'll be itching to get to work on everyone else's too. One of the greatest favours you can do for non-gardening friends and relatives is to help with their pruning. If nothing else, it's a far more enjoyable way of singing for your supper when dining out or staying for the weekend than washing up or helping with the bedlinen.

Tools and equipment

Sharp secateurs are an absolute must as bruised or split stems encourage die-back and attract disease. If your grip isn't all it could be, ratchet-action secateurs need only repeated light pressure on the handles to cut progressively deeper and deeper. If you are left-handed you should get hold of a pair of special left-handed secateurs. All hand tools should be comfortable to use.

Some gardeners, usually trade professionals, prefer to prune with a curved gardening knife. While they certainly give a clean and accurate cut if you've got the skill and the strength to use them correctly, they can be very dangerous in inexperienced hands. For thick stems and branches a small saw might sometimes be needed; gardening ones often take the form of a giant clasp knife.

previous page Pruning soon becomes a smooth and instinctive response to each plant's needs rather than a series of hectic fumblings based on quaint diagrams and gobbledegook text. Just observe through the seasons how your cuts affect growth and flowering – then dealing even with the much feared wisteria will be like falling off a log.

It makes sense to wear tough gloves and a heavy jacket to protect your hands and arms from scratching. You should seriously consider buying a pair of safety goggles. However silly you feel in cheap plastic specs from a DIY shop they beat a poke in the eye any day.

Why prune?

Basically, we prune for any or all of the following reasons:

- to cut out dead, damaged and diseased wood
- to admit light and air to the plant as a whole
- to remove any crossing, crowded or lop-sided stems
- to keep a plant within bounds
- to produce attractive new stems where we want them
- to create a pleasantly shaped, well-balanced tree or shrub
- to encourage the growth of new foliage
- to produce larger or more abundant blooms
- to produce larger or more abundant fruit

Light pruning

Light pruning can be done at any time of year to tidy up wind-damaged twigs and stems, to remove frost-damaged or sun-scorched leaves, or to remove the odd bit of diseased or pest-ridden plant material. This is often the only pruning needed by mature deciduous shrubs and most evergreens.

Deadheading – the removal of spent flower heads – also falls into this category. Deadheading diverts energy back into the plant to produce fresh growth and more flowers. Disparage it at your peril, unless you are planning to collect seed or you are saving seed heads either for their appearance or as a food for wildlife. Regularly deadheading roses throughout the summer to prevent the formation of hips promotes repeat flowering and is at least as rewarding an endeavour as the most expert hard pruning the previous spring or autumn.

Gently snap and twist off the flower head while pinching the stem between finger and thumb. Be careful not to damage any young buds in the crooks of the leaves below, as they will produce flowers in due course. Practice makes perfect and experienced gardeners deadhead at Olympic speed and more or less in their sleep.

For some plants such as catmint, ballota and *Stachys byzantina* you can adopt a more radical approach. Just give the whole plant a haircut with a pair of garden shears when the flowers start to go over. It will be flowering again in a few weeks.

More drastic still is a trick for refreshing tired specimens of gardener's garters (*Phalaris arundinacea*) when they start to look tired and shabby in high summer. Cut the whole lot down to the ground! In no time at all you'll have a stand of fresh young leaves to carry you through to autumn.

Well-judged intervention of this nature can produce all kinds of effects and helps build up an understanding not only of how plants grow but of how they can be made to grow according to your wishes. This will soon give you the confidence to tackle your first shrub with aplomb.

Hard pruning

By hard pruning we mean anything more than a little light snipping and snapping. Unlike light pruning, hard pruning involves cutting seriously into woody stems or branches, and often includes cutting out older wood and removing old branches.

Pruning clematis is nothing like the tangle it's made out to be. *C. tangutica* flowers in late summer on new shoots, so neeeds pruning in winter. Simple!

When to prune

Most hard pruning is carried out in spring – that is, when the worst of the winter weather is over and before plants start into spring growth. However, there are no hard and fast rules about when to prune and common sense should always prevail. You might have good reason to prune at other times of the year – in particular, autumn.

If you have a problem with wind, it is always worth giving a rough trim in autumn to such leggy shrubs as buddleja, elder, fremontodendron and lavatera so they don't damage their roots when rocking in gales. Cutting a good 30cm/12in or so from younger stems can be seen as a prelude to the proper spring prune. Where you are quite sure that you want to thin out old and tired stems, this is definitely the time to go ahead in a windy garden.

Before being too vigorous with autumn pruning – to avoid wind damage or for any other reason – it is worth remembering that the more of a plant you leave intact through the winter, the better it is protected from the ravages of frost. Not only is the base of the plant insulated by the leaves and stems, but the more stems the plant has, the greater your insurance against unforeseen damage. If you leave just two perfectly pruned shoots in autumn only to have them blasted by winter frost then you're well and truly stuffed in spring. Any compromise between protecting against frost and protecting against wind damage is simply down to instinct and common sense. Pruning too much too early can also stimulate precocious growth which will either be too tender to survive the winter, or which will be cut away anyhow in the main spring prune. Either way you're wasting both the plant's energy and your own.

If your garden is in a mild and sheltered spot, the logic is different and a hard pruning in autumn can be a positive boon. The earlier you prune,

Some shrubs that flower on the current season's growth

Generally these are best pruned in spring, but they may be pruned in autumn to avoid wind damage or encourage earlier flowering.

Abutilon
Buddleja davidii
Caryopteris
Colutea
Cytisus battandieri
Fremontodendron
Fuchsia
Indigofera
Lavatera
Leycesteria formosa
Perovskia
Phygelius
Sambucus

the greater your opportunities for an early and extended flowering season. Most roses, for example, have two main flushes of flowers and an early, or autumn, prune generally leads to an earlier first flush, which gives more time for a second flush to form. If a poor summer follows a late, or spring, pruning there might not be enough time after the first flush for a second flush to form. Prune late to shape a plant on a favoured site and you will find yourself cutting away quantities of healthy new growth which would have been put out elsewhere by the plant had you done your formative pruning in autumn. Wrong time, wrong result. If you can safely prune in late autumn, you're a very fortunate gardener indeed.

Most woody plants bloom straightaway on new shoots grown between spring and summer. That is, they flower on the current season's growth. These are pruned in spring, unless you decide to prune in autumn for the reasons just given. Simple.

However, we're now going to throw a spanner in the works. Some woody plants only bloom on stems grown the previous year. That is, they flower on last season's growth. For these, the timing is different and pruning is two-tiered. When blooming is over, in late summer or autumn, take all flowering stems back with a very light touch. Then dive in hard and take out about a quarter to a third of the old stems completely. The first step of this two-tier approach tidies up the extremities while allowing new growth to go through to a second year. The second step clears up congestion and promotes replacement growth from the base. If it has suddenly hit you with a thud why you've had nary a flower in years on your hydrangea, philadelphus, forsythia or whatever, the problem is easily solved. Leave it alone for twelve months then proceed as above. You'll have flowers within a year and in three to four years, depending on how much old wood you take out at a time, you'll have a totally rejuvenated specimen.

Some shrubs that flower on last season's growth

Generally these are best pruned immediately after flowering to allow as much time as possible for the formation of new growth which will bear flowers the following year, but in cold climates it is often wiser to delay pruning of late flowerers until spring.

Abelia
Buddleja alternifolia
Buddleja globosa
Callicarpa bodinieri
Carpenteria californica
Chaenomeles
Cytisus scoparius
Deutzia
Dipelta
Forsythia
Genista
Hydrangea macrophylla
Kerria japonica
Kolkwitzia
Philadelphus
Ribes sanguineum
Ribes speciosum
Weigela

How and where to prune

You'll be delighted to learn that knowing how and where to cut is the easiest part of the entire business.

Your aim is to cut at a bud or leaf joint where new growth will appear. You should cut on a shallow slant just above a bud. A sloping cut discourages rot by allowing rainwater to run away from the bud. If the cut is too close, the bud may die. If the cut is too far away, the surplus stem will die back – at best this looks ugly, at worst, it encourages disease. You should aim to make the top of the cut 5mm/½in above the bud. Make the lower edge of the cut just level with the bud, on the other side of the stem. If you are dealing with a plant whose buds form in pairs on opposite sides of a stem, you just cut straight across the stem above the buds. And there you have it, ladies and gentlemen.

You are aiming for a healthy, well-balanced specimen that is a suitable size for your garden and has maximum flowering potential. Whatever you're pruning, first cut out any damaged, dead or diseased wood. Dead stem tissue is brown or black in cross section – either way it is perfectly easy to recognize. You want to see only good, healthy tissue, which is generally cream or pale green in colour. Any awkwardly crossing stems should also be cut out, as should most inward-growing stems. By cutting stems back you encourage more vigorous development of lower shoots. An apparent paradox of pruning is that an unevenly balanced shrub is best reshaped by leaving the good side more or less intact and pruning vigorously into the weak side. Timid pruning is a far greater evil than wildly enthusiastic pruning, but if you are ever in any doubt about how far to go, it is always sensible to stand back and take a breather. You can always cut more off, but you can never put it back on again.

Rejuvenate a tired and overcrowded shrub by completely removing a quarter to a third of the old stems. As fresh new growth springs up from the base, more old wood can be removed in subsequent years.

Cut a single stem back to a strong pair of leaf joints and two new stems will grow from buds in these 'axils'. This is the key to producing bushy plants with maximum flowering potential.

Hedging

The occasional short-tempered hacking about simply won't do. It is an obvious yet rarely acknowledged fact that hedge trimming is a particular form of pruning and as such it deserves a little thought and care. Keeping a check on size is just one aspect of the business; good trimming also promotes strong dense growth which not only improves a hedge's appearance with age but considerably prolongs its life. A well-maintained yew hedge will outlive several generations of gardeners and privet can easily last a lifetime, but turn your back on a leylandii hedge for an instant and it will transform from quick filler to eyesore to menace before you can say the words 'boundary dispute'.

Most hedges are all the better for hard pruning at the outset, so if you ever have the luxury of planting one you should muster the courage to cut it to within 15cm/6in of the ground in the autumn of its first year. In the second and perhaps even in the third year all new shoots should be completely cut back again to the previous year's wood. This generates multi-stemmed growth from the base, which promotes good shape and uniform leaf coverage from top to bottom; it also allows for periodic regrowth as the odd stem suffers damage or dies back with age. Cowardly cutting in these formative years leads to bald spindly legs and flabby top-growth in middle age with little hope of a second flush of youth. Rejuvenate old, shabby or damaged hedges on a rolling basis by pruning a few old stems hard back to low buds each autumn. If they were properly trimmed from the outset this presents no difficulties; if not, cross your fingers and be prepared to plant afresh.

Coniferous hedges are handled a little differently. The leading shoot of each young plant should be left alone until the required height is attained; then the hedge should be 'stopped' by cutting a good 15cm/6in or more off the top of each leader. If the second aspect of the job is done properly this temporary drop in height will be restored later by bushy side growth. Regular trimming of side shoots is essential from the outset on even the tiniest of specimens since few conifers apart from yew can produce new leaf shoots from old wood. Conifer hedges well trimmed from year one develop thick green mantles capable of almost infinite regeneration. Unfortunately they are as rare as hen's teeth. Most are neglected in youth and grow to resemble nothing so much as ugly old rows of telegraph poles which they might just as well be for all that they respond to belated trimming or remedial pruning.

The best profile for all kinds of hedge is the traditional wedge or 'A' shape, preferably with a slightly rounded top. The gentle slope or 'batter' to the sides streamlines the hedge against lashing wind and rain and over

Thanks to the crisp greenery of the box edging, in winter-time and early spring when the herbs, flowers, fruit and vegetables are mainly noticeable by their absence, this beautifully laid out kitchen garden remains a visual feast.

For a tall coniferous hedge of yew or non-U leylandii, trim the sides regularly but leave the main stem intact until the desired height is reached.

Broad-leaved hedges such as box, hawthorn and privet should have *all* stems trimmed right from the outset to promote a firm network of dense bushy growth.

winter the narrow top prevents heavy snow from settling and splitting open the hedge under its weight. Work towards this ideal from the outset and simply let the proportions grow as the hedge matures. A hedge need rarely be wider than 60cm/24in at the base and should never be taller than you can safely and comfortably trim. Run a line of string along a hedge or move a template along as you go only if you're manic about a perfectly straight cut – otherwise your eye is quite good enough a guide.

Trim established evergreen hedges such as box, holly, privet and fast-growing conifers in late spring/early summer and once again in late summer or very early autumn. Deciduous hedges such as beech, hawthorn and hornbeam are best given a short back and sides while still dormant in spring, with perhaps a second lighter trim and tidy up in mid-summer. Yew is so slow-growing that only a single late-summer cut is necessary.

Should you be inclined that way, dense-growing, small-leaved hedging plants such as box, yew and the evergreen honeysuckle *Lonicera nitida* are excellent for topiarizing, either as free-standing specimens or as part of an existing hedge. Repeated light pruning over many years creates a complex and resilient network of tiny branching stems which can lead to the formation of animal forms or geometric shapes. Balls, for example.

Clematis

So much mystery and nonsense surround the pruning of clematis that many people are either scared to touch them or too frightened to grow them at all. We can't see what the fuss is about.

- Early small-flowered and evergreen clematis don't need hard pruning. Just give a light prune after flowering. This is a job for late spring or early summer.
- Early large-flowered clematis such as 'Nelly Moser' respond best to a light pruning in late winter or early spring. Only cut away a lot of growth if you come across either an old dead stem or a seriously ugly tangle.
- Late-flowering clematis need hard pruning in late winter or early spring. Cut each stem back to a pair of buds close to ground level.
- All clematis respond well to having their stems spread out to avoid kinking, and to deadheading, which encourages flowering.

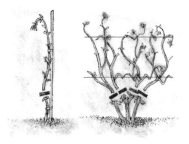

Courage! Hard prune late-flowering clematis each winter and ever more stems will arise from the base to produce masses of summer blooms.

Roses

Contrary to popular opinion, roses are perfectly easy to prune. For our purposes they fall into three categories.

- Climbing roses with woody stems need little more than a light trim any time between late autumn and early spring. Some climbing roses are referred to as ramblers. These usually send out long fleshy shoots from the base every year and need a different approach. Cut away all the old stems in autumn then tie in the new green ones in their place.
- Shrub roses like the old-fashioned *Rosa rugosa* need little thought. Just trim all stems back by a third between late autumn and early spring, and cut away dead wood. To encourage rejuvenation from the base remove one main stem completely every second year.
- Bedding or bush roses are the most commonly found ones. All new rose bushes should be pruned hard back to healthy buds no higher than 15cm/6in above ground level. Don't feel the least twinge of guilt about hacking off those lovely stems you've just spent good money on. You're being cruel to be kind. It gives the root system time to develop and encourages strong growth and more stems at the base of the plant. You get a tough, stocky and vigorous rose bush instead of a long, leggy weakling. If the old stems on established bushes are crowded, cut out a few completely between late autumn and early spring; and prune the remaining

Shrub roses are remarkably resilient to attack and make the ideal assault for new recruits to pruning. Cut all stems back by a third in winter and deadhead throughout the summer to prolong the flowering season.

main stems back to young buds anywhere between 15cm/6in and 30cm/12in from their base. The harder pruning gives fewer but bigger flowers while the lighter pruning gives a greater number of smaller flowers. If you cut further away from the base of each main stem than 30cm/12in, you're a big girl's blouse and your roses will look silly.

Shrubs grown for their stems

Many dogwoods are plain and unappealing for much of the year, but then they drop their leaves in winter to reveal brightly coloured stems that some people find attractive when there's not much else to look at. With these – or with shrubs whose stems have more subtle effects, such as *Rubus cockburnianus*, *Salix magnifica*, *S. udensis* 'Sekka', *S. alba* subsp. *vitellina* 'Britzensis' or *Stephanandra tanakae* – simply prune them hard and close to the ground in early spring. They will then grow a fresh new set of colourful stems to flaunt the following winter.

Wisteria

This flowers on short spurs which grow laterally from the stems. In this respect wisteria is like many fruit trees. The procedure for creating as many flowering stems on these spurs as possible is not difficult but it is different from anything we have encountered before. When flowering is over prune all new stems back to within six buds. This discourages long extension growth and encourages the plant to divert the rest of this year's energy to the buds instead. In early spring cut these same stems further back, now to within three buds of the main stem. This thwarts any plans the plant might have had to regrow from the new tip and you get the lateral or side growth in spring and the flowers in summer that you've been scheming for all along.

Prune a young wisteria by removing low-lying shoots while creating horizontal stems by encouraging side shoots to branch out at regular well-spaced intervals. Where it has filled out nicely, cut back any further new growth to form flowering spurs.

If you've got an old wisteria and it flowers poorly, this approach will quickly rejuvenate it. Don't panic if a young wisteria doesn't respond straightaway: wisterias can take up to seven years from planting to flower for the first time. In the meantime follow a more relaxed version of the above regime. Prune selected new growth lightly to train the plant into shape and prune the rest as described.

Suckers

It's pruning, Jim, but not as we know it . . . Suckers are shoots which spring from dormant buds in roots. They can be lifesavers, as when a plant is cut to the ground by frost, but on grafted plants they're a downright nuisance and must be ruthlessly excised. Not with your secateurs, though, as that would stimulate replacement growth. Excavate gently around the sucker to find where it is attached to the roots and pull it off at source. This will tear away any accompanying buds which would otherwise spring up in its place. If you haven't got the strength to do this by hand, use a claw hammer, levering the suckers as you would pull nails from wood.

Pruning fruit

Apples and pears

Apples don't come true from seed so nurseries produce named varieties by grafting growth from a parent tree on to a host rootstock. The vigour of the rootstock determines the ultimate size of the tree but its shape and its capacity to bear fruit are down to you and your trusty secateurs.

While a young tree is growing to maturity, prune leading stems in late winter to create an open and well-balanced habit with as many strong branches as possible. At the same time prune all new side growth hard to encourage the formation of short spurs which in a year or so's time will flower and bear fruit close to these weight-bearing stems. To create new spur systems and to enhance existing ones simply cut back all new growth on side stems and existing spurs to within six buds. Consider the weight of fruit these stems will have to bear and cut back weaker stems to within three buds; cut weak stems out altogether. That's it. Leave the tree alone until next winter. Just remember to admire the blossom in spring and to harvest the fruit in autumn.

After a few years of perfect pruning spur systems can get a little congested. As you see this happening thin out healthy ones a little and remove old and weak ones completely. You'll have more apples than you know what to do with!

A very few apple varieties, such as 'Irish Peach' and 'Worcester Pearmain', fruit at the tips of their shoots rather than from spurs and so need a different regime. Prune the leading tip of each main branch every

previous page On established apple trees high yields can be maintained for many decades with a pruning regime which creates new and more vigorous fruiting spurs to replace old and congested ones on a rolling basis.

winter to promote fruiting side shoots and to prevent the branches from being weighed down with fruit at the ends. At the same time remove a proportion of older wood entirely to make way for young replacement growth, preventing the tree from developing too lax a habit.

Apricots, cherries, plums, nectarines and peaches

All stone fruits are vulnerable to infection through cuts in their stems. To reduce the risk they are pruned not when they are dormant in winter but when the sap is rising in the spring. To determine the precise moment, wait until you see the first new buds breaking through. Spur pruning is unnecessary; your only interest is to create an open, well-balanced specimen.

Because these trees are so disease-prone, any suspect growth should be cut away as soon as you see it, whatever the time of year. Old wood that is dead but not diseased can be removed with minimal stress to the tree in late summer when it can be clearly identified. If you leave it until springtime when the tree is more or less bare you might just make a mistake and amputate the wrong limb.

Blackberries and raspberries

Blackberries are related to roses and should be pruned like rambling roses.

Prune summer-fruiting raspberries this way too. With autumn-fruiting raspberry varieties, prune all the canes to the ground between late winter and early spring.

Blackcurrants

Because they don't fruit on the current season's growth, you need a mixture of old stems, young stems and developing stems all at the same time. In late winter to early spring, cut any branch which has borne fruit

back to a healthy new side shoot and remove a few of the oldest stems altogether to promote fresh growth from the base. Generally speaking older stems are recognizably thicker than younger ones and have darker bark, but mistakes can be made. So much for the theory. If you can't get your head round all this, or if like us you simply can't be fagged, don't despair – there are two ways to skin the rabbit. Established blackcurrants are such thugs that they can be pruned with impunity while still in active growth, so you might just as well prune as you harvest. When a stem is chock-full of ripe fruit in summer just cut it away and strip off the currants while sitting at the kitchen table. This is far less back-breaking and involves no thought whatsoever. If you've got the luxury of several bushes, an equally idiot-proof approach which guarantees a full yield simply involves cutting alternate specimens to the ground each winter and cropping the unpruned ones the following summer before cutting them down in their turn. Take your pick.

Figs

Fruit forms continuously on new growth as shoots develop. In hot countries this gives a long cropping season but in cold countries you're lucky to get any edible fruit at all. The only figs with enough time to ripen are late developers which overwinter as tiny embryos and therefore have all of the following spring and summer to catch enough sun. Fruits which form in spring and summer have already missed the boat and, too soft to overwinter, they fall to the ground in autumn. Prune hard in early spring

Originating in China, apricots run riot in the Near and Far East but are so prone to silver leaf and die-back in cooler climates that pruning is as much about removing diseased wood as promoting young fruit-bearing growth. The musky-scented flesh of wall-ripened fruit such as these makes it all worthwhile.

to establish an attractive framework and to clear congested stems. Prune again lightly in summer, taking all new shoots back to within six leaves.

Gooseberries, red currants and white currants

Gooseberries are sold as bushes on a short stem or 'leg'. If you can be bothered they can be pruned to form spurs in the fashion of apple trees and wisteria. In mid-summer prune all new side shoots back to buds about 10cm/4in from their base, but leave the leading growth alone. In late winter prune the leaders back by half their length, remove tired old stems completely and cut the summer-pruned laterals back to 5cm/2in. This system will produce a modest crop of large fruit and is often used for dessert varieties and gooseberries for exhibition at shows. If you want really large ones, crop every alternate fruit in late spring or early summer (cook them if they're ripe enough) and leave the remainder to ripen into monsters. But is it worth all the effort?

An easier approach, and the one we recommend, is to treat them like blackcurrant bushes on sticks and prune once in late winter or early spring. You'll have slightly smaller fruit but a much bigger crop.

Prune red currants and white currants in the same way but take all new side shoots on mature specimens back to one bud.

Grapes

A grapevine is usually grown as a permanent rod which can become thick and knobbly with age and is pruned annually to produce long lateral shoots on which the clusters of fruits form. The laterals are tied along parallel wire supports running at a right angle to the central rod. In the very dead of winter and at no other time whatsoever cut each lateral back to one bud. Never prune back to an inward-facing bud – rub it away with your fingertip and prune to the next outward-facing one instead.

And now for a grave warning. If you prune a grapevine at the wrong time of year, after the sap has started to rise in mid-winter, it can bleed uncontrollably and even die. Mild bleeding can be staunched by applying a piece of raw potato. Failing this you might try cauterizing it with a red-hot soldering iron. Better still, don't let it happen in the first place.

Nuts

'A woman, a dog and a walnut tree, the more you beat them, the better they be.' Formerly, high branches on walnuts, almonds and sweet chestnuts were crudely pruned from ground level by whacking off their growing tips with a big stick to encourage more profuse lateral growth, or so the saying goes. Such modern luxuries as ladders and secateurs have rendered the custom obsolete but the general principle prevails: establish a well-shaped, well-branched tree, and then leave well alone when it grows beyond your reach. Mature trees crop quite heavily enough without further resort to violence.

Cobnuts protrude from short-tailed leafy husks but 'full beards' enclose filberts; loosely termed hazelnuts, these are the only nut trees to crop reliably in colder climates and the heaviest yields come from specimens grown as shrubs. Commence pruning when the tiny red female flowers are out in spring. Hazelnuts are mainly borne on the upper part of young stems, so cut last year's nut-bearing branches back to generate young shoots. Remove the older wood completely to maintain an open habit and promote basal regrowth. Cut all remaining stems back to their outermost female flower. Where stems only bear catkins, the male flowers which fertilize the crop, wait until the pollen fades and then cut them clean away. In late summer prune long vigorous shoots back by half but leave twiggy growth untouched. This gives the right balance of male and female flowers next spring ready for another fine crop next autumn.

Keeping the enemy at bay

Creepies and crawlies and long-legged beasties
stalk the undergrowth and
bring the dreaded lurgy on their wings.
To a healthy garden
they are as water off a duck's back.
Let Nature preen your garden
by enlisting the local wildlife,
experimenting with companion planting
and generally nurturing a balanced ecosystem.

Pests and diseases

Inviting friends and family round to share in the fruits of your labours is one of the great pleasures of gardening. But there are other far less welcome visitors to contend with. The devil has many disguises and the two-horned nightmare, pest and disease, haunts the gardener in many forms.

We don't recommend using chemical sprays in the first line of defence. In fact we don't recommend them at all. Not even as a last resort. This is not because of woolly-minded liberalism – in fact, the squeamish among you will baulk at our hands-on approach to creepy-crawlies. No, it is down to sheer common sense. Using chemical sprays – both against actual infestation and against the chance of infestation, as is so often recommended – simply poisons the vegetables you are growing and then yourself in turn. There is also a long-term threat to the environment from the general build-up of chemical toxins.

Most insecticide sprays are multipurpose: they kill all the insects they come into contact with, harmful and beneficial ones alike. Some of the most virulent pests, aphids for example, are relatively simple creatures. If conditions are right for them, they breed and multiply rapidly and many generations are spawned in the course of a year. But their natural enemies, predatory insects like ladybirds and damselflies to name but two, are larger and more sophisticated souls. Their life cycles are measured in months and years, not days and weeks. Spraying might give you immediate psychological satisfaction and offer effective short-term relief in the

previous page You wouldn't hand round insecticide as a condiment at table, so why spike your food with it in the garden? There are safer ways of keeping caterpillars down and if they do have the odd cabbage dinner at your expense they generally leave quite enough behind for you.

garden, but in the long term it doesn't solve your problem at all; it simply makes it worse. The pest population can recover quickly; the predator population can't. Your problem will come back with a vengeance and you will have to face it all by yourself this time. Things spiral out of control: a greater and greater reliance on chemicals leads to a greater and greater imbalance in the natural order of your garden.

Preventative spraying certainly can't be regarded as equivalent to inoculation, as it promotes immunity not in the crops but in the pests. It is more on a par with the misuse of antibiotics like penicillin in animal farming – the effect is that when disease really strikes it is resistant to treatment. Because of the widespread use of pesticides in recent years, many pests have developed an immunity to the chemicals we use against them. Whitefly in particular are now so pesticide-resistant that manufacturers are even admitting as much on their packaging.

When the balance of Nature is upset it finds a way to compensate. When business is threatened new ways must be found to improve the bottom line. Stimulated just as much by necessity as by public demand, the wheel is now turning full circle and many organic and biological controls are being touted as alternatives to synthetic pesticides. These too should be approached cautiously.

Pyrethrum (*Tanacetum cinerariifolium*) is a good example. The plant itself is an attractive member of the *Asteraceae* family. Its dried and powdered flowers have been used as a natural pesticide for years. It kills by paralyzing the nervous system of insects. All insects, that is. Harmful ones and beneficial ones alike. It also kills fish. That's not all. Natural pyrethrum is harmless to mammals but the commercially extracted active ingredient (also, but rather disingenuously, called pyrethrum) is toxic. To quote Alexander Pope again, 'Who breaks a butterfly upon a wheel?'

So how do we best proceed?

Remedies

There are a number of interesting and perfectly harmless curative and preventative measures against insect, fungal or bacterial attack.

Attack may well be a symptom of some underlying problem with a plant. The plants most vulnerable to attack are the ones under stress. First ask yourself how you can improve conditions for an ailing plant.

Is the plant in the right place? Siting plants where they will thrive, an art we have already discussed, will make them stronger and better able to withstand attack. For example, a hosta wilting for want of water or from too much sun will be an easy target for slugs and snails. Transplant it to a cooler, shadier spot or one with a more moisture-retentive soil and once it recuperates the slimeballs will be off to find something easier to get their teeth into.

Poor soil conditions can lead to nutrient deficiencies, which weaken a plant and leave it vulnerable to attack. Soil enrichment is a long-term process, but in the short term, fast-acting natural fertilizers such as seaweed extract or a liquid feed made from comfrey leaves can help.

Buy disease-resistant plant varieties. Nurseries and seed companies promote a wide range of plants and seeds that have been selectively bred to resist attack. Encourage them, not the pharmaceutical giants who produce chemical sprays.

In the vegetable garden, crop rotation prevents the localized build-up of pests and diseases, as does the prompt consignment to the compost

When stressed or on a poor diet plants are as vulnerable to attack from pests as people are prone to catching colds. Like vitamin pills, slug pellets are excellent short-term palliatives but no substitute for a healthy lifestyle. Grown in decent soil in an open shady border – the conditions foxgloves and hostas like best – these strapping lads can look after themselves.

heap of the roots and leaves left behind after harvesting.

Wallflowers and stocks are of the *Brassicaceae* family and can act as hosts to the fungus which causes club root in brassicas. Don't grow them in an ornamental kitchen garden with sprouts and cabbages.

Whitefly find the colour yellow irresistibly attractive. Roll squares of bright yellow card into tubes and wind clear adhesive tape around them with the sticky side out. Hang or stake these tubes around infested plants and the whitefly will soon come to a sticky end.

Earwigs eat leaves and flowers to rags by night then sleep off their supper by day. Stick small plant pots stuffed with dried leaves and lawn clippings upside down on short poles around affected plants. The earwigs will treat these as beds. Every day or so tip the contents out on to some paving and stomp on them. Make up fresh beds as you go.

Cabbage root flies lay their eggs in the soil around plants and when the maggots hatch they crawl towards the stems and eat them. There are two chemical-free solutions. Fit a saucer-sized piece of cardboard around each young plant. The flies will lay their eggs on this instead of in the soil; exposed to the elements they will dry up and die. Alternatively, wrap a narrow strip of aluminium foil about 15cm/6in long around each stem before planting out. Start as low down in the root system as you can and wind an overlapping upward spiral to the base of the leaves. As long as you plant with at least 2.5cm/1in of foil above ground the maggots haven't got a chance. A belt-and-braces approach is to combine both techniques.

The best, simplest and most overlooked approach is: when you see a problem, remove it by hand. It's so obvious, but nobody does it. When you see a few aphids on your roses or some caterpillars on your cabbages, do you run off to look them up in a book or do you squish them between your fingers? At the first sight of scale insects do you reach for your spraygun or do you scrape them away with your thumbnail? The heel of your boot is faster-acting and far more eco-friendly than a box of slug pellets (unless hurled with great force) and swift surgery with your secateurs is the simplest way of treating damaged tissue on trees and shrubs. Where only leaves are affected, simply pick them off and burn them or bin them.

If you think you've got a lot of slugs and snails, just wait until after dark, when they come out to feed, and hunt them down by torchlight. You'll be horrified to see how many you've really got. Gather them up and dispose of them as you will. If foxes are regular nocturnal visitors to your garden, leave the slugs and snails in a pile and they'll be gobbled up with relish. If not, squish them all or else your work will have been in vain. Once you've tried this you'll never again waste your time trapping the odd slug or two in saucers of beer or under orange skins. However it is still worthwhile scattering sharp grit or crushed eggshells around seedlings or particularly juicy-leaved plants in order to make the going tough for them.

Vigilance is the key word. Nip a problem in the bud and it will never grow into a crisis.

Always keep an eye out for the least sign of attack as pest handiwork is easier to spot than the culprits themselves. Dull, thin and distorted leaves sound the alert for sap-suckers like aphids, mites and whitefly, while freestyle chomping is the hallmark of caterpillars, beetles, slugs and snails. Fungal infections like mildew and rust often follow hard on the heels of physical attack and cause leaf curl and withering. Most insidious of all, root damage by leatherjackets and vine weevil grubs shows only as a general malaise before a plant wilts dramatically and gives up the ghost.

125

Weeds

One man's weed is another man's wildflower. Keep the ones you like and pull out the others. You might consider using the leaves of edible ones as salad greens.

If you need to clear a patch of virgin ground or a particularly weed-infested area that has been out of cultivation for some time, here is an effective, foolproof and entirely natural method. In late winter double dig the plot to bury the weeds deep underground and then sow a crop of late-season potatoes. These are often described as a cleaning crop, but the real work is done by you. Digging to sow, hoeing to earth up and forking over to harvest all help kill off old bits of the weeds' roots and germinating weed seedlings. The potatoes help smother seedlings with their leaves but the bonus is the crop itself which gives you something to show for your labours.

Smothering your weeds with old carpets, the curious preserve of some misguided New Age hippies, is not to be recommended. Carpets, like the poly-styrene blocks, old tyres and fridges full of CFCs that also litter some gardens, leach harmful chemicals into the soil as they degrade. Don't mistake wombling for organic gardening.

Weeds coming from under the fence from your neighbour's garden are easily dealt with. The simplest way to deter them is to run a line of plastic or metal edging strips along your side of the boundary. You can also use old slates or roofing tiles; just insert them 15cm/6in below ground level with at least 10cm/4in sticking up to guard against wandering roots and spreading stems.

If you're feeling adventurous or if you're wary of damaging the roots of a hedge you can fight fire with fire by using invasive garden plants to your own advantage. Why defend when you can attack? A stand of montbretia or goldenrod planted slam-bang up against the boundary will soon be marching next door to crush the enemy. A good rule of thumb is to use plants that are thriving well on one side of your garden against the weeds from your neighbour on the opposite side. Finding themselves deprived of their preferred conditions, they will grow to find them again in your neighbour's garden. For instance, deploy a few divisions of white rosebay willowherb (*Epilobium angustifolium* var. *album*) from your sunny side to your shady side and they'll be bombing next door to your neighbour's sunny side in no time. Conversely, the shade-loving lily-of-the-valley (*Convallaria majalis*) manoeuvred into position beneath a sunny hedge will be itching to go undercover as soon as possible.

Eat your weeds

The French have been cultivating dandelions for years. The Vilmorin Catalogue of 1885 includes such gems as Pissenlit Mousse (moss-leaved dandelion), Pissenlit Amélioré à Coeur Plein (thick-leaved or cabbaging dandelion) and Pissenlit Amélioré Très Hatif (improved early dandelion). We thoroughly recommend taking a leaf out of their book: the following weeds are not only perfectly edible but are quite delicious when added to salads. Eating your garden snails is an altogether different matter . . .

Bistort `(*Persicaria bistorta*)
Chickweed (*Stellaria media*)
Common orache (*Atriplex patula*)
Common wintercress (*Barbarea vulgaris*)
Daisy (*Bellis perennis*)
Dandelion (*Taraxacum officinale*)
Fat hen (*Chenopodium album*)
Good King Henry (*Chenopodium bonus-henricus*)
Ground elder (*Aegopodium podagraria*)
Hairy bittercress (*Cardamine hirsuta*)
Lamb's lettuce (*Valerianella locusta*)
Miner's lettuce (*Claytonia perfoliata*)
Shepherd's purse (*Capsella bursa-pastoris*)
Sow thistle (*Sonchus oleraceus*)
Wild sorrel (*Rumex acetusa*)

Gardening on the wild side

Don't stop at using garden plants against weeds. You can use them against insects as well. Pitcher plants and Venus fly traps aren't necessary; marigolds do nicely instead. Simply by having plenty you tempt helpful insects in to keep your pest population down. The nectar in African, French and pot marigolds (*Tagetes erecta*, *T. patula* and *Calendula officinalis*) attracts adult hoverflies and wasps in quantity. Hoverfly larvae eat aphids at a rate of about five hundred a week each! Different parasitic wasps lay their eggs in aphids and caterpillars as a convenient source of food for the larvae when they hatch. They eat up their living hosts from the inside out then emerge through the skin as adults. All quite disgusting if you're a mummy aphid or a cabbage white butterfly, but rather gratifying to the gardener.

Other plants can be used to repel or confuse pests – members of the *Alliaceae* family being best known for this. Garlic, onions and chives have all been proved to put carrot flies off the scent when grown alongside carrots.

We hope this natural approach has set you thinking that if Nature itself were allowed into your garden perhaps it would be a happier and healthier place still. It would. A garden pond with shallow sides will attract frogs and toads who will eat slugs and snails. A few wildflowers dotted in the lawn will bring in butterflies and bees. A bird bath and a well-stocked bird table will bring an assortment of useful and colourful visitors. When you lose a few strawberries to the blackbirds think about those on your plate saved from slugs by the thrushes. When the sparrows peck your crocuses watch the finches on your teasels. The benefits of a natural approach far outweigh the disadvantages and your pleasure in your garden is the greater.

The flower garden

Talk the talk and walk the walk.
With botanical terms tripping lightly off your tongue,
combine advanced colour theory
with the fundamentals of good design
to make a personalized garden
with year-round impact.
Go on! Create the garden of your dreams.

The ideal garden is a miniature ecosystem of well-adapted plants laid out in a harmony of scent, colour, form and texture according to your individual artistic vision and fulfilling all practical considerations with regard to maintenance and to optimum use of space. An impenetrable jungle lies at one extreme, a stark prison yard at the other. The happy medium is somewhere between the two, but precisely where it lies is up to the individual. You. Fads and fashions may come and go but it's your garden and it's your taste that counts, your skill that shows.

Most gardens offer a variety of growing conditions and from the hottest, most exposed terrace to the darkest and dampest nook you already know how to exploit each situation to the full. That in itself makes all the difference between a mediocre garden and one aspiring to brilliance. A little more knowledge about choosing and placing plants will put you on the fast track to attaining the garden of your dreams.

Plant names simplified

A rose by any other name would smell as sweet but could be hard to order from a catalogue. Common names of many plants vary from region to region and country to country: one man's bistort is another man's snakeweed, a Scottish bluebell is an English harebell. Therefore the universal gardening language of botanical Latin ensures that we all know what we're talking about, in this case *Persicaria bistorta* and *Campanula rotundifolia*. Far from being élitist, anachronistic or downright affected,

previous page Never mind all that minimalist nonsense. Most of us prefer homes with furniture, music with a tune, paintings with colour and poetry with rhythm. And we respectfully suggest, to the fools who think otherwise, that flowers are essential to every garden.

it's a practical necessity that's simple to follow and often surprisingly descriptive and useful. Common sense and a pocket dictionary tell you just as well as a classical education that *Campanula rotundifolia* is a little bell with round leaves, that *Gypsophila paniculata* likes growing on chalk and bears loose clusters of flowers, and that *Amorphophallus bulbifer* might not be to every maiden lady's taste.

Plants usually have two italicized names, giving general guidance with the genus then specific information with the species. Thus *Rosa* is a rose is a rose but *Rosa gallica* is a species native to France, Turkey and the Caucasus. Variation within a species takes many guises. *Rosa gallica* var. *officinalis* is a naturally occurring variety brought into gardens, commonly called among other things the apothecary's rose and the red rose of Lancaster. *Rosa gallica* var. *officinalis* 'Versicolor', commonly called Rosa Mundi, is a red- and white-striped cultivated variety, or cultivar, specially selected for its distinct characteristics and artificially maintained by careful propagation. For convenience's sake, once selective breeding complicates or more or less obscures a plant's origins the genus is followed simply by a vernacular cultivar name, saving it the tedious fate of Welsh tourist attractions, German nobility and babies christened after football teams. So the distinguished *Rosa* 'Gloire de France', a fragrant lilac pink Gallica descendant, and such bastard spawn of Beelzebub as *R.* 'Rock 'n' Roll' and *R.* 'Tequila Sunrise', are equal under the rules of botanical Latin if not in the eyes of the beholder.

When two species are crossed to produce a particularly notable hybrid the new strain is marked with an ×, as when *Camellia japonica* and *C. saluenensis* produced *C.* × *williamsii*. Interspecies hybrids are quite common in flower gardens and legion in fruit or vegetable plots but so far only a few intergeneric hybrids have occurred within plant families. In the *Araliaceae* family *Fatsia* and *Hedera* are the proud parents of × *Fatshedera* and in the *Cupressaceae*, × *Cupressocyparis* has sprung up from *Cupressus* and *Chamaecyparis*. So much for Mother Nature and the patient dabblings of nurserymen. By the time genetic modification really complicates the issue no doubt we'll all have grown two heads to keep up.

Horticultural jargon

Certain words and phrases recur often enough in garden-speak to warrant clarification. Horticultural jargon might seem like a descent into madness but it's nothing more intimidating than a useful form of shorthand to help you assimilate information quickly when choosing plants for your garden. Brace yourself for a little dictation.

An annual is a plant which completes its life cycle in a year. Annuals grow from seed in spring, flower in summer and set seed in autumn, which then lies dormant over winter before giving rise to the next generation – marigolds being prime examples. Possibly the most confusing plants to get to grips with, biennials generally live for two years, putting on green growth first of all then flowering and setting seed in the second year. Foxgloves and verbascums are typical garden biennials. If you allow biennials to set seed they'll always have a place in your garden, albeit a different one each time. To guarantee continuity of biennials, plant *or* sow in two successive years or plant *and* sow in one. This way you'll always have a mixture of developing and flowering specimens. It's possible to eke an extra year out of many biennials by deadheading scrupulously, but this is at the expense of next year's seedlings. Some particularly durable biennials may even be regarded as short-lived perennials. True perennials go on and on for years and years, hardiness permitting.

Hardiness is a term relative to location and is best thought of as a plant's ability to withstand winter wet and cold. Some plants grown on a

Like many biennials, sweet rocket or Dame's violet (*Hesperis matronalis*) is a prolific self-seeder which scents the air beautifully and fills out borders a treat.

cold eastern seaboard might never see the year out and so be regarded as tender, yet similar specimens might thrive at the same latitude in a warm westerly location and be regarded as fully hardy. A plant might well prove hardier on a well-drained northern hillside than in a waterlogged southern frost pocket. In short, common sense and local knowledge are as valuable in determining hardiness as the arbitrary guidelines in books. Be daring. Many plants are hardier than cautious writers lead you to believe.

A hardy annual can complete its life cycle outdoors. A half-hardy annual might need kick-starting in a greenhouse or on a warm windowsill. In cold climates many tender perennials are often treated as half-hardy annuals – otherwise they would need winter protection from frost which might necessitate bringing them indoors. To play entirely safe with tender perennials, shrubs and trees, treat them as houseplants and conservatory or greenhouse specimens.

Generally speaking, the soft growth of herbaceous perennials dies back to the ground entirely each winter, while trees and shrubs, which are woody perennials, retain their stems. If they are deciduous, they lose their leaves all in one go at the end of each growing season. If they are evergreen, they keep their leaf cover throughout the year but shed older leaves regularly. Most people fail to notice this but if you stand in the middle of a pine plantation you can actually hear the pitter-pat of needles (which are in fact leaves) falling to the forest floor. A shorthand exists within the shorthand, and in gardening circles perennials are assumed to be herbaceous unless specified as evergreen and the perennial nature of woody plants is taken for granted. And the longer we live on this Crumpetty Tree the plainer than ever it seems to be . . . Nurse, the screens!

Planting

Before turning to flowers in their broader garden context where plant material is just one part of the overall concept, let's look at the simple art of digging holes and planting plants.

First put your containerized plant into a bucket and fill it with water to cover. This ensures thorough wetting of the rootball before planting. The bigger the hole the better – it should be at least three times as wide and twice as deep as the pot, and it is worth recalling the old dictum of a shilling hole for a penny plant. Fill the hole with water and allow this to seep away as you mix organic matter, such as compost or well-rotted manure, and perhaps a slow-release fertilizer, into the excavated soil. With the plant still in its container to minimize root disturbance, lower it into the hole to assess how much soil needs tipping back in to to get the neck of the plant level with the surrounding ground. As you do this, scrape away the top 1cm/½in of soil from around the plant into the bottom of the hole to get rid of any weeds and weed seeds. If you need to drive in a stake to support a tree or a tall shrub, do it now to get it to the greatest depth possible. Tip in soil to the appropriate level and finally knock the plant out of its pot; gently loosen any congested roots before putting it in and filling around the sides with more soil. Firm the earth gently to a little below ground level and use the remaining earth to form a ring or reservoir around the hole. Water the plant liberally and when it has all soaked away draw the rim of dry soil gently over the wet surface to act as a water-retaining mulch. Add a further mulch of compost or leafmould if you wish, but leave a healthy gap around stems to prevent rotting. You're done. If this seems a bit of a performance, watch the results. You'll be amazed. The soil is light, friable and freshly enriched with humus and nutrients; your plant will be racing to get its roots into it.

Design

Your garden is a stage where you, your family and your friends act out a variety of roles. A small garden is like a studio theatre where the space must be versatile, the props are lightweight and minimal, and the scenery is used to establish a tone rather than to steal the show. A large garden is like a grand old opera house where one backdrop gives way to another, where each act takes place in a different and fully realized location, and where the performance is rounded off by some amazing *coup de théâtre*. On a warm summer's evening in an urban backyard a rotary clothes drier might be uprooted to make room for a game of boules on the gravel. When darkness falls, a round folding table and chairs might appear as dinner is served by fairy lights or candles. For a lunch party on a scorching weekend the table might be stuck through with a giant canvas parasol firmly anchored in the slot vacated by the drier. Everyone is as happy and content as the house guests on a rolling country estate in a parallel universe where drinks are served on the terrace, croquet played on the lawn, light suppers are laid out in the conservatory and the laundry is done below stairs. Laying out a good garden is about engaging and delighting the senses with whatever means we have at our disposal. It is a privilege open to us all.

One of the earliest conceits in western gardening was the medieval knot garden where low hedging such as box was formed into patterns to please the eye with shape alone. Occasionally the 'knots' would be filled in with herbs and what few flowers were in cultivation. Later elaborations

With colour in the foreground, an arch to frame the view and a large pot to draw the eye, this side entrance is more than just a pathway. It extends a warm welcome and entices the visitor into the garden proper.

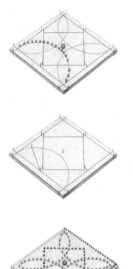

There's no need to get your knickers in a twist when laying out a knot garden. Use strings and stakes to mark straight lines and form curves with a giant peg-and-twine compass. Just stick one peg in the ground and scratch out the desired arc with the other. The longer the string, the gentler the curve. Highlight 'woven' designs with hedging plants of contrasting colours such as wall germander or cotton lavender.

included 'weaving' the hedges together by cutting one intersecting hedge higher than the other and using different-coloured hedging; brightly coloured gravels were also employed to give a marquetry effect. If all this can be achieved with an evergreen hedge, some flowers and a bit of gravel, it's no wonder that the modern gardener, hundreds of years on in time, and spoilt for choice, often doesn't know quite where to begin.

Planning on paper is a necessity for the skilled professional working off-site, who has to give precise instructions to craftsmen and labourers. But amateurs and not-so-skilled professionals can soon lose sight of reality, indulging in wishful thinking while overlooking the obvious. A beautifully drawn and coloured-in planting plan might be a work of art in its own right but in the real world it will be far less satisfactory than a bed arranged lovingly and imaginatively over time and *in situ*.

You might lay out the most amazing garden in the world only to realize too late that it's best appreciated not from your own sitting room but from the attic window of your neighbour. Also, something that seems important in theory might be of no real significance in practice. An ugly coal bunker or oil tank might be given so elaborate a screening treatment with antique treillage as to draw the eye ineluctably to the very thing it's supposed to conceal, when common sense, a coat of paint and a few shrubs would have worked wonders. People can spend a lifetime doing bizarre things with trees, walls and fencing to blank out ugly surroundings and never come to the simple realization that a beautiful garden is the ultimate distraction. Do you want to be congratulated on how well you've hidden the gasworks with a thumping great conifer as visitors stand in its shadow in your tiny backyard, or would you rather your guests sat on a white wooden bench beside your *Cornus alternifolia* 'Argentea' captivated by the *Cyclamen coum* f. *albissimum* growing through the *Hedera helix* 'Sagittifolia Variegata' beneath it? You could have a nuclear power station going into meltdown behind you and they wouldn't even notice.

Learn how to lead the eye and the spirit where you want them to go. Thoughtful styling can make a narrow garden seem wider, a small garden bigger, a large garden more intimate, a formal garden more inviting. Run a lawn the width of your garden with a deep border at the bottom and compared to a lengthwise lawn edged with two narrow borders it will transform the view from the house and the feel of the space will be quite different. A path laid diagonally will be longer than one laid square on and will introduce a dynamic note to a garden, producing shapes which widen and narrow. A serpentine path carves out a long, circuitous and scenic route, a straight path the shortest and most efficient one. A rough pebble surface slows you down, hard stone spurs you on. Bricks laid lengthwise draw the eye forward and lengthen perspective; widthwise they shorten perspective and draw the eye sideways to admire adjacent plantings. A pebble mosaic and a bubbling fountain might distract your attention from noisy surroundings; a chamomile lawn and a limpid pool will induce peace and tranquillity. A focal point in a billowing cottage garden such as a statue, an urn or some topiary gives the eye a focus and somewhere to linger a while; loosely planted blooms in an otherwise unrelentingly formal garden give respite to the soul.

Planting design

Gardeners can employ subtle tricks in planting design. Flowers and leaves can exaggerate or mitigate the effects of their surroundings. The austerity of a modern minimalist 'garden' can be heightened with a few well-placed architectural forms (bamboos and phormiums) or eclipsed by a lush traditional planting. A plant used as a feature in one part of a bed or garden can be used elsewhere to complement a more dominant one. Where two massed plantings adjoin, the boundary can be blurred by mixing in a few specimens of one plant with the other – this works beautifully with apparently naturalized plantings of bulbs and in borders where subtle graduations of colour are required. Odd numbers of plants always look better in informal plantings, perhaps because the eye finds it harder to impose order. Even numbers invariably produce formal effects,

Good bone structure carries beauty into old age. Simple topiary and a fine brick path enchant and animate this winter garden long after the summer blooms have faded.

even where they're not intended.

Again, because the mind is always seeking order out of chaos it tends to assume that things that look alike are the same size, so plants of a similar shape but a different size can be used in tricks of scale and perspective. A lake planted with *Gunnera manicata* on the near shore will look more expansive with *Rheum palmatum* on the further shore because the smaller clumps of rheum are read by the mind's eye as distant stands of the much larger gunnera. In another trick of perspective, an avenue of trees will appear longer if the further trees are progressively smaller and longer still if the trees are planted closer together and the road narrows. Even when we really know better we just can't resist reading real landscapes as perspective drawings.

Small-scale trickery can be far more subtly deceptive when done well. A border will seem longer from one end if large-leaved plants give way to small, but shorter from the other end as small ones give way to large. Where flowers are concerned, reds and strong warm colours thrust themselves forwards while blues and soft misty pastels visually recede. To enhance the length of a lawn in spring it could be planted with large clumps of large-flowering bright yellow daffodils close to the house gradually mixing with then making way for progressively smaller but closer-together clumps of dwarf lemon yellow narcissi. Simultaneously, white crocuses could give way to tiny late-flowering snowdrops. The beds or borders could slowly take over the deception by being predominantly red closer to the house, gradually shifting away into purples and paler and paler blues. Massed tubs close up could be echoed in the distance with a few scattered pots. Large-leaved trees and shrubs at the start of your diagonal or serpentine path could lead the way to finer, daintier specimens at the further end.

Colour and form

There are no rights and wrongs when it comes to combining colours but a little theory goes a long way towards achieving any desired effect. The workings of our eyes affect our perception of colour and this in turn affects the related vocabulary. Pure sunlight contains all the colours of the rainbow, arbitrarily described as red, orange, yellow, green, blue, indigo and violet, although the real range of hues is infinite since each one shifts imperceptibly into another in progression along the spectrum. But we are simple souls and our eye cells only register three essential colours: red, yellow and blue. All other colours are perceived as combinations of these three, the easiest to spot and to name being those composed in equal parts of two 'primary' colours, the 'secondary' colours. Red and yellow make orange, yellow and blue make green, blue and red make violet. Less run-of-the-mill colours tend to be described either as further combinations – greeny-blue, orangey-yellow, or by drawing analogies – wine-red, turquoise, saffron.

Colours lying adjacent on the spectrum make for relaxed and harmonious plantings since the eye need only register a series of gentle transitions. To explore this approach imagine a thin slice of rainbow bent round into a wheel so that violet merges into red. Adjoining colours and their near neighbours on either side work well together: lime greens, yellows and oranges have a certain affinity; reds, purples and blues combine beautifully; purples, blues and greens through to emerald have distinct allure. It's interesting to note that some combinations seem lighter and brighter, and others richer and darker. This is because each colour has an intrinsic tone, yellow and orange being the brightest, blue and purple the darkest, red and green somewhere in between.

A given colour can also range through any shade, from the most translucent of pastels through its purest most densely saturated essence

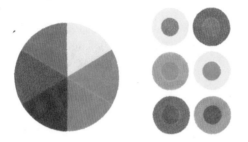

Studying a colour wheel reveals all kinds of subtleties. Note how spots of orange, green and purple look brighter against their lighter-toned neighbours and softer against the darker-toned ones.

before receding almost to black in dark, muted tones. Clearly, the opportunities presented by selecting a narrow colour palette are as varied as they are fascinating. A garden can be illuminated with gold, dissolved in a haunting sea of blue or transformed into a lush green oasis. The psychological effects of colour should not go unregarded: the 'warm' colours from yellow to magenta are generally stimulating; the 'cool' colours from lime green to violet are soothing – restful. If you have a personal passion for a particular colour or range of colours, indulge yourself. The practical benefits of this approach to the budding gardener are that unity and integrity are achieved without the least risk of discord and all the while your familiarity with plants and your confidence with colour is growing and growing.

When you feel ready for adventure, try juxtaposing colours from opposite sides of the spectrum, which contrast sharply. Red and green, yellow and violet, blue and orange – each partner makes the other one sing. This is so visually exciting because not only is each one as far as possible from the other on the spectrum but as far as the human eye is concerned each 'complementary' colour is registered by all remaining cells not activated by the other. Sensory overload! Orange is made up of the primaries red and yellow, so is as far removed as possible from blue. If you

Contrasting plant forms and simple colour combinations are skilfully juxtaposed: the yellow achillea glows against the softly billowing purple cotinus, its horizontal flowers in counterpoint with the soaring crocosmia leaves, its colour reprised in the foreground rudbeckias.

look at an orange flower for a while your blue sensors won't come into play at all but your red and yellow ones are stimulated to the full. If you then look quickly at a white wall or a sheet of paper, you'll see a phantom shape of the bloom, but in blue. The white wall, reflecting all the colours of the spectrum, registers more strongly on your blue sensors than your tired red and yellow ones. Try this experiment with any flower you fancy and you'll realize that after looking even briefly at any colour we are physiologically predisposed to see its complement. The canny gardener takes full psychological advantage of this simple fact. Just as a blue flower looks more intensely blue next to an orange one because the eye is already primed to see it, so the plumes of red astilbes look reddest against lush green foliage and golden yellow roses really glow when underplanted with blue-purple lavender or nepeta.

Plants don't just come with differently coloured flowers, leaves, berries and bark, they come in a variety of sizes, shapes, textures and habits lending form and substance to the gardener's colour palette. If a garden is a work of art it is as much a piece of sculpture as a painting.

Large single flowers contrast beautifully with clusters of small ones, narrow leaves are the perfect counterpoint to round ones, filigree foliage billowing gently in the breeze provides a subtle foil for strong-growing plants with stark architectural outlines. A dense, close-textured shrub is all the more imposing planted beside a willowy and ethereal one, a delicate fern daintier still against a solid backdrop. Dumpy mounds cry out for vertical accents. Strong contrasts in form can be softened and unified by loose interplanting. Foreground harmonies of shape and colour can be reworked with taller plants behind and further echoed with a background of shrubs, climbers and trees.

Even if you work largely by instinct, you can always learn from others. Looking at plantings you admire in other people's gardens and analysing why you think they work successfully helps clarify your own ideas about what really makes a garden tick. You can jot down names and steal ideas wholesale; you can adapt plantings to your own garden conditions and according to personal taste; you can note fleeting impressions of colour and form and recreate them using entirely different plants.

With hard-won experience you can achieve stunning effects in an instant, using the principles we've described, and plant up an empty bed in one go from scratch. In the meantime, we recommend a step-by-step approach. Why plan a garden poorly when you can allow it to evolve beautifully and learn as you go?

Buy something you like, dig a hole and put it in. Stand back and look at it. Your personal reaction to the plant *in situ* now dictates what happens next. Let's imagine the chosen specimen is *Cistus ladanifer*. It's a large Mediterranean shrub, so you put it to the back of a dry sunny border. After a week of admiring its papery white flowers inordinately you're off on another trip to the garden centre where you're irresistibly drawn to the maroon velvet Moss rose 'Nuits de Young' with its strangely textured stems and buds. Only when you take it home and plant it do you realize it's the same rich deep red of the central blotches on the cistus petals. Something's happening! You're so pleased with this detail that it's not until a few days later that you stand back and notice, with a little disappointment, that your two adjacent shrubs have roughly the same form and habit. You need a contrast and find the solution in a few soaring verbascums with huge grey velvet leaves and some round hummocks of cotton lavender for the foreground. Coincidentally, the yellow flowers of these two pick out the yellow hearts of the cistus and the rose. This is so exciting that you splash out on a pot of *Achillea filipendulina* 'Gold Plate' with its horizontally borne yellow saucers of massed tiny flowers. Suddenly there's too much grey foliage, so you buy some dark shiny

bergenias for the very front of the bed, some green and bronze fennel for filling in and a fig tree and some golden hops for the wall behind. The bronze fennel encourages you to round out the colour of your rose with a vigorous honey-scented *Buddleja davidii* 'Black Knight' and the dainty chocolate *Cosmos atrosanguineus*. You build in turn on the charm of the cistus with hastily bought pots of *Digitalis purpurea* f. *albiflora* and annual *Gypsophila elegans* 'Giant White'.

Congratulations. You're a gardener, and a good one too. In the course of a few weeks you've created a fantastic summer flowerbed which you can develop further as the seasons progress and as the years pass by. You can also apply the lessons you've learned to different effect in different parts of the garden. You might want to go wild with colour or create an elegant all-white border. Perhaps you're captivated by scent or fascinated by texture. Whatever you want to achieve, start off with one or two keynote plants and take it from there. Combine colours perfectly by buying plants in full bloom and ensure year-round interest by spreading your purchases over a year. Just let each successive plant you put into the ground sow a seed of imagination in your mind and you simply can't fail.

previous page Hot borders bursting with vibrant colour are psychologically stimulating and make excellent visual pick-me-ups for large gardens. However, the eye soon needs a rest, so this kind of planting should be used with caution in smaller settings.

Professional help

You could go an altogether different route and bring in outside help. But if you do, beware.

We applaud the many excellent professionals working in garden design today. But we are concerned by the way elements of sound professional design are trickling down to the mass markets in a debased form and ruining many a decent garden in the process. Worse still are the nasty piles of tat knocked together in a weekend and passed off as gardens by way of magazine or television entertainment. Such third-rate design is nothing for you to aspire to. Whatsoever.

Although creating a garden needn't be expensive, it can be if you employ a professional designer. The real money in professional garden design lies in hard landscaping. Raw materials can be bought at trade prices and marked up to retail and beyond for the client's benefit. A generous profit margin is added to the labour costs of sub-contractors and supervision might be extra. All this comes on top of a hefty design fee.

In comparison with hard landscaping, plants come pretty cheap – for professionals (who therefore make less money on them) and for amateurs. It is interesting to note that while many professionally designed gardens keep plants to a minimum and are awash with bricks, glass, concrete, stone, decking, raised beds, walls, fences, trellis, gewgaws, knick-knacks and doodahs, amateurs invariably concentrate on plants. And why not? After all, plants are what a garden's all about.

Creating a good garden requires hard work, careful thought and sensitivity. But a garden created without professional help will reflect its owner's tastes more truly than one created with help, and the pleasure it brings will be more satisfying for being its owner's own achievement. It could be yours.

A gardener's calendar

*'A work of the busiest pains is
by this little instrument rendered
the most facile and agreeable,
as by which you shall
continually preserve your Garden
in the perfection of beauty and lustre.'*
– *John Evelyn*, Kalendarium Hortense, *1664*

There is always work to be done in the garden but it changes in nature with the ebb and flow of the seasons. And each succeeding year is different from the last. That's what makes gardening so enjoyable. It does, however, mean that you should be guided as much by your own judgment as by any hard and fast set of rules.

We live in a busy world and time is precious. In truth many jobs are better done as the fancy takes you and when leisure permits than when performed grudgingly against the clock. We offer the following calendar in this spirit. Treat it as a guideline to deviate from and you won't go far wrong – *Deo volente*.

Some jobs, such as propagation and lawn maintenance, are so seasonally based that we introduce them here for the first time; others have already been touched on and are mentioned here as prompts. A few snippets are added simply as icing on the cake.

Late winter

Finish pruning apple and pear trees. Prune your roses, according to your location and the weather. Cut the stem dogwoods *Cornus alba*, *C. sanguinea* and *C. stolonifera* to the ground (this can also be done in early spring). Give late-flowering clematis a hard pruning and give early-flowering large-flowered clematis such as 'Nelly Moser' a light trim. Prune hydrangeas. In the kitchen garden, take your secateurs to blackcurrants, red and white currants, gooseberries, hazelnuts and autumn-fruiting raspberries but keep their different requirements firmly at the front of your

previous page Its last few hips shining through the hoar frost, *Rosa moyesii* is as welcome a sight on a crisp winter's morning as when its stems arch under a mass of bloom at the height of summer.

mind. Prune blackcurrants like raspberries at your peril — a moment's confusion can cost a year's harvest. Give deciduous hedges a good trim before spring growth starts.

Lawn sites should be prepared now. Dig the ground thoroughly and remove large stones; then use a rake to level it off and remove any small stones at the same time. Lightly firm the soil by systematically shuffling your feet over the surface in the manner of an old-age pensioner walking

Prune rose bushes hard back in their first year to promote a hearty root system. In subsequent years remove weak and crossing stems and take out dead, damaged or diseased wood. Shorten the remaining stems to within 30cm/12in of the ground.

The coloured shoots of shrubs grown for winter effect should be cut back almost to their point of origin. Brand new shoots arise from the old stems and fresh basal stems spring from the ground. On congested specimens remove some old stems completely before pruning back the remaining shoots.

on black ice. Leave everything to settle for a month before sowing later.

Finish all heavy digging and soil preparation which has been post-poned since autumn due to sloth or inclement weather. Top dress trees, shrubs and climbers with manure or compost. Country-dwellers can infuse a few sheep droppings gathered on Nature rambles in a bucket of water to make 'tea' which can be diluted and used as a liquid feed until you switch to comfrey later in the year.

Indoors, the first stage in rejuvenating poinsettias for next year is to cut them down to within 8cm/3in of soil level. Should the cuts bleed pro-fusely, cauterize them with the flat of an old table knife heated in a gas flame for a moment or two.

Plant out chitted seed of early potatoes. Plant or divide as necessary rhubarb, horseradish and seakale so that their crowns are just level with the ground and mulch well. Jerusalem artichokes are an effective wind-break in the kitchen garden if not at the table; plant tubers 8cm/3in deep and 30cm/12in apart in staggered rows. Lift and divide clumps of chives and the perennial onion *Allium fistulosum*. Shallots are the easiest of all onions to grow and highly pest- and disease-resistant. Plant them 20cm/8in apart with their noses showing – pulling off the papery tops keeps birds from tugging them out for fun.

Sow tomatoes under glass and consider sowing the following outdoors if the weather isn't too harsh: broad beans, early beetroot, summer cab-bage, salad onions, parsley, parsnips, swedes and turnips.

Crops in season include Jerusalem artichoke, broccoli, Brussels sprouts, cabbages, cauliflower, celery, endive, kale, leeks, spring onions, parsnips, salsify, scorzonera, swedes and turnips.

Blooming their hearts out as winter turns to spring, hellebores and snowdrops are some of Nature's most subtly coloured and gracefully formed flowers.

Early spring

Finish pruning your roses, and prune shrubs like *Buddleja davidii* which flower on young wood. Lightly prune wisterias back to within three buds on stems cut back to six last year. Give figs their hard spring pruning and prune stone fruits when their buds break.

To rejuvenate shabby old ivies take them right up against their support with a pair of shears, then use a broom to clear dead leaves, dirt and creepy-crawlies from the nooks and crannies. In a month or so's time the bare stems will be covered with a fresher, flusher sheet of green leaves.

Transplant and divide herbaceous perennials, retaining young growth and discarding hard old stems and roots. This requires the patience of Job and the judgment of Solomon. Large woody hosta and peony crowns might need cutting back with a knife. Slice them as you would divide a cake between three or four greedy people, not as you would cut doorsteps from a loaf of bread. Sow marigolds, mignonette, Shirley poppies, sunflowers, sweet peas and any other hardy annuals you fancy. To save the bother of transplanting, scatter the seeds where you want them to flower. Plant gladioli and montbretia in holes three times as deep as the corms are round. Plant bought snowdrops 'in the green' and divide and transplant

Use a piece of wood to make shallow rows in a tray of moist compost before tapping seeds gently out of their packet. Sift with a fine layer of dry compost and cover to help prevent water loss and to maintain as even a temperature as possible.

overcrowded ones when flowering is over and the leaves are yellowing at the tips. They resent disturbance enormously, so keep as much soil around the roots as possible and don't split them more than once every four years.

Sow new lawns on prepared sites, first raking the surface to level out any dips and bumps and to raise a light tilth. To distribute the seed evenly broadcast half of it working from the far end of the site to the near end; then scatter the balance working from one side to the other. Rake the seed in gently; then lightly firm the soil with the head of the rake before watering thoroughly. Deterring birds is only for the anally retentive as the lawn will be perfectly all right even if they do have the odd snack. The lawn will be well established by mid-summer; until then keep foot traffic to a minimum except for weeding. Resow bald patches on existing lawns and fill shallow depressions by sifting successive thin layers of sifted soil over them at fortnightly intervals. This is the last opportunity for speed merchants to lay turf, but the job is really best done in autumn.

Indoors, if they usually live on a windowsill, bring clivias into the body of the room as they burst into bloom. Indoor flowers look washed out against the light with the sun shining through them. Positioned with the

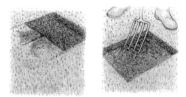 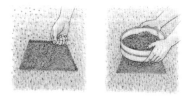

To reseed a badly worn patch of lawn, remove the damaged turf, fork over the ground and top it up with a mixture of soil, sand and compost. Sow with grass seed and cover with a fine layer of sifted soil; then water gently but generously.

light streaming on to them and reflecting off the petals, their colours appear more vibrant and intense. Bear this in mind as other houseplants come into flower. Tidy up fast-growing houseplants like daturas, pelargoniums and sparmannia or the African lime with scissors or secateurs. Propagate new houseplants by taking cuttings and trimming them of leaves then cutting 8cm/3in lengths of stem just above and below a leaf node and inserting them halfway into fresh compost, three or four to a pot to save space. Pot up anything which has outgrown its container.

Allotment holders and kitchen gardeners can now sow with abandon. Only use whole packets of seed in one go if you've got a lot of mouths to feed. Otherwise stagger smaller sowings over a couple of months to ensure successive cropping. Take your pick from early beetroot, broad beans, Brussels sprouts, summer cabbages, cauliflowers, early 'stump-rooted' carrots, leeks, lettuces, onions, parsnips, peas, spinach beet and summer spinach. This is a good time for sowing herbs. Continue planting early potatoes and plant onion sets between now and the middle of spring. Chit seed potatoes of mid-season and late varieties.

Broccoli, cabbages, cauliflower, kale, leeks, spring onions, rhubarb, salsify, scorzonera, seakale and summer-sown spinach beet are yours for the taking. Cabbage and turnip thinnings provide 'spring greens'.

Mid-spring

Finish hard pruning shrubs which will flower on this year's growth. As their blooms fade begin light pruning of early-flowering shrubs such as chaenomeles, flowering currant, forsythia and kerria to promote the growth of new wood which will flower in subsequent years. Trim evergreen shrubs only if they need a little reshaping but prepare to give evergreen hedges, with the exception of yew, their first cut of the season.

The sight of a well-pruned apple tree bursting with blossom
in the spring is a reward for hard work past and a promise
of things to come.

Reserve any drastic action for worn-out old laurel bushes and hedges, which can be reinvigorated now or in autumn by cutting them back to 30cm/12in from the ground. As a precaution against failure, laurel cuttings the size of cut flowers root easily indoors in jugs of water.

As new shoots emerge on herbaceous perennials remove all remaining leaves and stems left over from last year.

Ignore any advice to apply lawn fertilizers or wormkillers unless you're the groundsman for a bowling club. Most lawns are seriously over-fed and worms help aerate them. Begin regular mowing of established lawns but don't set the blades lower than 3cm/1½in and don't use a clippings box. Longer grass is less prone to drought and even healthier for a regular mulch of fine clippings at the roots. Don't mow new lawns until the grass is at least 5cm/2in high.

Remove seed heads on spent daffodils so that leaf energy goes into fattening bulbs for next year and not into seed production. Take note of overcrowded clumps to lift and divide later this year for better flowering the next.

In the vegetable garden, elaborate on the system of successive sowing by combining early, mid-season and late vegetable varieties. For example, if you start sowing maincrop carrots now and make a couple more repeats of early stump-rooted ones, your carrot harvest, which begins next month when you commence cropping your early spring sowing, will continue well into winter. Begin sowing winter brassicas and maincrop beetroot, and experiment with unusual vegetables such as globe artichokes, cardoons, endive, Florence fennel, kohlrabi, salsify and scorzonera. Artichokes and cardoons can also be grown from young plants or divisions, but the other odd-bods are best sown *in situ*. Remember to sow fast-growing catch crops of radish and lettuce between rows of slow growers.

Put tomato plants and young cabbages in their final positions. Plant onion sets, mid-season and late potatoes, and earth up the shoots of new potatoes. Mind your back.

If you've got the aforementioned patience of Job, sow asparagus seed now to begin cropping in four years' time. Otherwise buy one- or two-year-old crowns, and plant them 30cm/12in apart and 10cm/4in deep with the roots spread out around them like spiders' legs, and they'll be cropping in two or three years. Rich soil and good drainage are essential. One route to the latter is to plant over a trench filled with champagne bottles.

Crops in season include broccoli, spring cabbage, cauliflower, kale, leeks, lettuces, spring onions, rhubarb, seakale and spinach beet. Thinnings of root crops make delicious baby vegetables.

Late spring

Remove suckers on flowering cherries, fruit trees, lilacs and roses as you see them. Appraise new growth on roses and other ornamentals and prune out anything inappropriate like crossing stems or thin weedy shoots.

Push in twiggy sticks around tall herbaceous perennials. As the plants grow they hide the supports and retain a degree of flexibility in the wind.

Shoots arising from the rootstock of grafted trees and shrubs require urgent attention. Trace them back to source with a pair of old secateurs but *on no account use these in a conventional way*. Proceed like a dentist using pincers on bad teeth and *pull* the suckers clean away. The longer they're left intact the more they sap a plant's energy and the harder they are to remove.

This is a far better approach than strapping plants to canes or encircling them with nasty wire doodahs.

You can also pinch out growing tips of flowering herbaceous perennials to promote bushiness and keep height in check. This puts flowering back by a week or two, so a clever ruse to achieve a continuous and extended flowering season is to pinch out alternate plants, deadhead full-height ones after flowering to promote a second flush, and continue deadheading into late summer as the shorter plants come into bloom. Plant up hanging baskets and window boxes and plant out summer bedding from the garden centre if you are not sowing annuals yourself. Put out young plants grown from root cuttings earlier in the year and sow more hardy and half-hardy annuals for late summer colour. With so many young plants and so much tender growth around, keep an eagle eye out for insect pests.

Plant out cyclamen corms, dahlia tubers and lily bulbs. Wait until the roots are showing on cyclamen or you might plant them upside down. Cyclamen and dahlias prefer shallow planting; lilies go deep. Some lilies root from the base of their stems as well as from the bulb so the deeper they go the better. 'Funny bulbs' – corms, tubers and rhizomes (many irises for example) – generally prefer shallow planting. Straightforward flower bulbs (anything which looks remotely like an onion) are a doddle: plant them in holes three times as deep as the bulb is round and if in doubt plant them deeper.

To make indoor cyclamen flower again the coming winter

plunge their pots up to the rim in a shady part of the garden until autumn. Mist spray houseplants occasionally to keep insects at bay. Throughout the growing season give them a dilute liquid feed each time you water.

Repeat sowings of early vegetables and add maincrop beetroot, turnip and swede for the coming winter, and sow courgettes, marrows, pumpkins and squashes when all danger of frost is gone. Sow runner beans beside the poles they'll grow up and sow sweetcorn in clumps to encourage pollination and the formation of cobs.

Earth up potatoes as necessary. Start pinching out sideshoots on tomatoes. Place a straw mulch around strawberry plants to conserve water, and to keep fruit clear of the soil and away from slugs.

Crops in season include asparagus, baby beetroot, broccoli, cabbage, early carrots, lettuce, spring onions, radish, rhubarb, seakale, spinach, spinach beet and early bunching turnips. Don't harvest asparagus until two or three years after planting or at least four years after sowing. Cut 5cm/2in below ground, making an oblique cut with an old bread knife. If you had enough champagne bottles when preparing the bed you'll be using a specially serrated asparagus knife instead.

Early summer

When the blooms are gone, prune evergreen clematis like *C. armandii* lightly and tidy up early-flowering small-flowered varieties of clematis such as *C. alpina* and *C. macropetala*. Prune broom. Trim hedges now and perhaps again at the very end of summer. With hedges as with women's hair, a few really good cuts are more effective than a lot of little trims. With lawns as with men's hair, frequent cutting looks better and is more practical.

It is about time to mow any grass through which daffodils were growing and to lift and divide any congested clumps noted earlier in the year. As a rule of thumb allow seven weeks from the end of flowering before starting either job; otherwise the bulbs mightn't have sufficient energy to flower next year.

Propagate shrubs and climbers taking cuttings or layering. Young plants produced by layering are remarkably hale and hearty because they continue to feed from the parent while putting down roots of their own. After a year, dig the youngster up, cut its umbilical cord and plant where

Sever a cutting from its parent plant just above a leaf node; then trim it to just below the next node up. Remove its lower leaves and dip the bare part of the stem into hormone rooting powder before poking it into a pot or tray of compost.

To propagate by layering, take a low-lying stem, remove the leaves from the part to go underground and nick the bark on the underside to stimulate root formation. Peg the stem down into the soil, water and if necesssary stake the end to keep it upright.

you will. Propagate tender perennials by taking cuttings. Sow seed of biennials and perennials.

Flowers for the home should be cut when they are already half out and only in the early morning before they lose water through transpiration. If you know in advance which plants you'll be picking from, give them a thorough watering the night before.

Earth up potatoes a little at a time and on a smaller scale begin to blanch the bases of leeks. Plant out winter brassicas in their final positions, taking appropriate preventative measures against cabbage root fly. Leave a few strong runners on healthy strawberry plants for propagation later but remove all other runners, so as to focus the energy of the established plants into producing fruit. Scrape earth away from shallots with your fingertips to ripen off the bulbs by exposing them to fresh air and sunshine.

Thin out young fruit on trees as you see fit. Gradually stop cutting asparagus and allow the shoots to grow into leafy stems which will provide energy for producing new crowns. In England, asparagus cutting stops as Ascot starts. This is a convenient opportunity to collect champagne bottles for drainage.

Continue sowing vegetables and throw in a few French beans. The kitchen garden will be burgeoning with asparagus, broad beans, carrots, cauliflower, fennel, kohlrabi, lettuces, spring onions, onions, peas, new potatoes, radishes, rhubarb, spinach, spinach beet, turnips, cherries, gooseberries, raspberries and strawberries. Pick crops when they're young and succulent. Men get obsessed with the size of their vegetables; women are more interested in what they can do with them.

Mid-summer

Prune philadelphus, weigela and wisteria after flowering. Shape figs and fruit trees trained as cordons, fans and espaliers. Remove apricot, plum and cherry branches affected by silver leaf and summer prune gooseberries only if you've opted for the complicated way of growing them. Deadhead flowers and squish insect pests as you pass through the flower garden. Take note of congested herbaceous perennials which aren't flowering as well as they might, with a view to dividing them in autumn or spring. Lift and divide bearded irises every three years, discarding old rhizomes or replanting young ones so they sit on the ground. Cut off the top halves of the leaves to reduce transpiration and minimize root rock. Plant autumn-flowering bulbs like *Nerine bowdenii*, autumn crocus and colchicum.

Pot up individually the rooted cuttings taken earlier in the year.

Apart from spring cabbage, only sow vegetables which will crop quickly – *tempus fugit*. Begin earthing up celery and earth up Brussels sprouts

previous page *Rosa* 'Magenta', dianthus and lilies harmonize beautifully, scenting the air and providing old-fashioned romance.

if necessary. Mulch runner beans. Help flowers set beans by spraying in the evenings with tepid water, but don't bother if there are lots of bees to pollinate for you. Peg down your selected strawberry runners in small pots plunged in the bed. This prevents any root disturbance when the time comes for transplanting.

Do your best to keep up with crops of globe artichoke, beetroot, broad beans, French beans, runner beans, broccoli, carrots, cauliflower, courgettes, kohlrabi, lettuces, marrows, onions, peas, potatoes, pumpkins, radishes, spinach, squashes, greenhouse tomatoes, turnips, apples, blackcurrants, red and white currants, gooseberries, loganberries, pears, plums, raspberries and strawberries. Give away whatever you can't eat rather than let it go over.

Late summer

Prune hydrangeas now or in cold climates leave them until the end of winter. If you can get the bulbs, it's not too early to plant daffodils, especially for naturalizing in lawns. Plant bulbs in grass up to twice the normal depth to allow the turf to grow unimpeded and for compaction by foot traffic, and to prevent mower damage.

Complete all hedge trimming and give yew its once-a-year cut. Later trimming can produce soft autumn growth susceptible to winter frost.

Sever rooted strawberry runners from their parents and plant them 30cm/12in apart in a freshly prepared bed. The later you plant them the more you reduce their cropping potential for next year. Plant them later than the middle of autumn and you shouldn't allow them to crop until their second year. Get a move on or brace yourself to pinch out a lot of flowers early next summer.

Collect and dispose of windfalls. Left on the ground they are prone to

disease and infestation which can spread to the fruit trees and bushes themselves. The best way to get rid of windfall apples too bruised for cooking is to cut them in half and put them on the lawn for the birds. They'll scoff them in no time and it distracts them from the fruit on the trees.

Along with spring cabbages, onions for over-wintering, winter spinach and spinach beet, there's still time to sow a few quick crops such as radishes and lettuces. Blanch cardoons by wrapping old newspapers or black bin bags around their stems.

In the kitchen garden you've never had it so good. Crops include globe artichoke, broad beans, French beans, runner beans, beetroot, broccoli, cabbage, carrots, cauliflower, celery, cucumbers, endive, kohlrabi, lettuce, marrows, onions, peas, potatoes, radishes, shallots, spinach, sweetcorn, tomatoes, turnips, apples, apricots, blackberries, blackcurrants, cherries, red and white currants, loganberries, melons, mulberries, pears and plums.

Early autumn

Prune rambler roses, blackberries, loganberries and summer-fruiting raspberries and tie in the new growths afterwards. Bending long shoots horizontally and training short ones sideways encourages the production of flowering and fruiting side shoots. This, incidentally, is why rigorously trained fruit trees bear such heavy crops in proportion to their size.

If you want to rearrange or divide any herbaceous perennials you have a small window of opportunity while the earth is still warm and before the

'Let the Frenchman have his Pear, the Italian his Fig, the Jamaican may retain his farinaceous Banana and the Malay his Durian, but for us the Apple.' – Edward Bunyard, *The Anatomy of Dessert*, 1929

If possible divide fibrous-rooted perennials gently with your bare hands. Otherwise prise them into smaller clumps with two opposing garden forks. Woodier roots and fleshy crowns are best tackled with a sharp knife or even a small handsaw.

weather gets cold. Moving early-flowering plants in autumn gives them more time to put out roots before diverting their energy into top-growth. Late flowerers are best left until spring in cold climates or on heavy soils but can be moved in autumn on light soils and in warmer climes. New plants grown from divisions in freshly prepared soil will be greener, healthier and more vigorous than their parents if not quite as tall in the first year.

This is especially noticeable with tough but hungry feeders like solidago and epilobium which deplete soil nutrients quickly given the chance but which can plod on in moderate condition for years. This is the best time of year to plant or transplant trees and shrubs. Dead leaves and stems of herbaceous perennials can be cut to the ground any time from now onwards, or you may prefer to leave them intact until spring as frost protection for roots and shoots.

Finish planting daffodil bulbs and start on crocuses, hyacinths and tulips. Plant in layers to get a really dense show of blooms without overcrowding the bulbs. Plant one layer deeply, almost cover the bulbs with soil, and then plant the next layer between the noses of the first. Another way to benefit from this technique is to plant early- and late-flowering varieties together to get a succession of blooms from a single site. Think carefully before mixing species though: early crocuses can be planted over late tulips but if you plant Dutch crocuses over daffodils they'll be hidden from sight and smothered to death.

For indoor use plant crocuses, hyacinths and narcissi in shallow bowls of bulb fibre. Water the compost, wrap the bowls in newspaper and then put them somewhere cool, dark and airy for a couple of months. Hyacinths may be grown in glass hyacinth vases in water alone, but be sure never to let the water touch the base of the bulb or rot will set in.

Bring back into the house any pots of cyclamen you plunged outdoors earlier in the year, repotting them if necessary.

Poinsettias need fourteen hours of darkness a day to produce flowerbuds (their 'petals' are actually coloured leaves – the real flowers

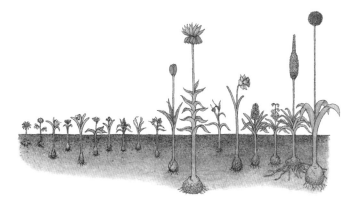

Planting depths for bulbs depend on the bulb size and flowering height of the plant. Tall specimens depend as much on their underground stems for stability as on the anchorage of their roots.

are the tiny yellow centres). Cover them with paper bags for the requisite length of time or keep them in a guest bedroom, closing the curtains early in the evening and opening them late in the morning. Christmas cacti benefit from similar treatment.

There's nothing much to sow besides brassicas. Continue earthing up celery and leeks. Lift maincrop beetroot, carrots, onions and potatoes and store them out of the frost and away from mice in a cellar, garage or shed. Pick all remaining tomatoes. Half-ripe tomatoes are more likely to ripen in a brown paper bag with a ripe one in amongst them than lined up in rows on windowsills. Use green ones for chutney or compost.

Eat, freeze, preserve and give away as much as you can. It's mean and stupid to leave crops until they're past their best. On offer this month are globe artichokes, French beans, runner beans, beetroot, broccoli, cabbage, cardoons, carrots, cauliflower, celeriac, celery, cucumbers, endive, kohlrabi, leeks, lettuce, marrows, onions, parsnips, peas, potatoes, pumpkins, radishes, shallots, spinach, squashes, swedes, sweetcorn, tomatoes and turnips. Fruit includes apples, apricots, blackberries, figs, grapes, melons, nectarines and peaches if you're lucky, pears and raspberries.

Mid-autumn

Take hardwood cuttings from ornamental shrubs and soft fruit bushes by poking 15–30cm/6–12in lengths of stem 8–10cm/3–4in deep in the ground. They're the easiest cuttings to take but the slowest to root; don't disturb them for a year or two.

With a haunting, elegaic beauty, whitebeams hold their autumn-tinted foliage well into winter. As the leaves dry out they curl in on themselves to reveal their characteristic silver-grey flipsides.

Grass goes into dormancy between now and the end of winter. Give the lawn one last cut and put the mower away scrupulously clean and well-oiled in readiness for next year. Lay turf between now and early spring on sites prepared as for seed. The sooner you lay it the longer it has to settle into its new surroundings and you'll find that turf delivered now reaches you in much better condition than turf lifted in cold weather. Seed may also be sown in autumn but it can take quite a hammering from the elements – we recommend waiting until spring even though this involves a little extra weeding and watering. Damage to edges of lawns can be repaired now by cutting out a generous piece of turf and turning it round so that the freshly cut inner edge presents flush to the edge of the lawn. Fill the gap at the opposite end with soil, firm it all down, and by the middle of spring even you won't be able to see the join. Get rid of hollows in lawns by lifting the turf and sifting soil underneath to the required height before firming it back into place. Don't overdo the soil or you'll have a burial mound instead of a grave. Minor depressions can be adjusted easily in spring but lumps are a bugger.

Finish planting hyacinths and tulips outdoors and plant or divide

Year-old stems are the best subjects for hardwood cuttings. Make a slanted pruning cut just above a good strong bud. Then cut straight across the stem just below a leaf node near the base. Bed the cuttings in firmly, as air pockets cause rot.

clumps of lily-of-the-valley. Check whether indoor bulbs need watering. Plant forget-me-nots, winter-flowering pansies, primulas and wallflowers. Tulips with forget-me-nots or wallflowers are classic plant combinations. Hyacinths and pansies work well if you get the colours right.

Pick all remaining apples and pears. Store perfect fruit only by wrapping them individually in paper and packing them in single layers in shallow boxes. The least bit of bruising or damage can quickly lead to rot so eat the worst fruit first.

To ensure an ongoing supply of fresh mint, plant up several pots with a generous quantity of finger-length cuttings from underground runners. These should lie 5cm/2in below the surface of the compost. Bring the pots on slowly in a greenhouse or frost-free shed; then force the mint as required by bringing it into your nice warm kitchen a pot at a time.

Finish earthing up celery and leeks and plant out in their final positions any remaining young winter brassicas.

Crops include Jerusalem artichokes, broccoli, cabbages, carrots, cauliflower, celeriac, celery, endive, kohlrabi, leeks, lettuces, parsnips, peas, salsify, scorzonera, spinach, turnips, swedes, almonds, apples, figs, grapes, hazelnuts, medlars, pears, plums, raspberries and walnuts.

Late autumn

Bush, climbing and shrub roses should be pruned between now and springtime according to your location. Begin pruning fruit trees too. Prune ornamental shrubs against root rock on exposed sites but don't touch any that bloom on old wood. Tidy up perennials by cutting back dead leaves and stems.

Paint, stain or creosote sheds and fences. Store garden furniture under cover with a view to painting it or applying linseed oil when it is thoroughly dry. Lag outside pipes against frost and turn taps off at the inside stopcock, being sure not to leave any water between them which could lead to bursts in freezing weather.

Don't leave any stakes or poles in the ground over winter. If you store them away they'll last for years and you won't poke your eyes when digging.

For – you knew this was coming – this is the time of the year when you must dig, dig, dig and dig again . . .

Sow broad beans and hardy peas. Harvest Jerusalem artichokes, Brussels sprouts, cabbages, cauliflower, celeriac, kohlrabi, leeks, parsnips, spinach, salsify, scorzonera, swedes and turnips.

Winter

A time for odd jobs rather than grand schemes. Savour your leisure – it won't last long.

As the weather permits, prune roses, grapevines, apple and pear trees as you see fit. Prune last year's growth on indoor climbers such as passionflowers and plumbago back to 15cm/6in or to within three or four new buds. You will never have such easy access for cleaning, repairing and repainting the inside of a conservatory as now – make the most of the opportunity.

Every few years gently scrub the trunks of ornamental cherries with mild soapy water to clean away green algae and old bark. The results are dramatic and attractive; *Prunus serrula* in particular will shine like a

Never underestimate the vestigial charm of dead stems and seed heads. Why feel bound to tidy them away when they can give solace in the cold months ahead? Jerusalem sage (*Phlomis fruticosa*) in winter is the epitome of shabby chic.